All My Springs

All My Springs

Journey of A Lifetime

C.L. Evans

authorHOUSE®

AuthorHouse™
1663 Liberty Drive
Bloomington, IN 47403
www.authorhouse.com
Phone: 1-800-839-8640

All characters and places in this book are true except for "The Traveling Heart." In some stories names have been changed to protect the innocent and the guilty. I would like to expressively convey to you (the reader) that I have no intentions to defame, purge, humiliate and hurt someone's person or feelings.

Published by AuthorHouse   08/25/2012

ISBN: 978-1-4772-4893-5 (sc)
ISBN: 978-1-4772-4892-8 (e)

Library of Congress Control Number: 2012913125

Spend time with books and people that you love.

Could a greater miracle take place than for us to look through each other's eyes for an instant?—Thoreau

To my son Derek I lovingly leave this written legacy. I pray it will become a source of pride and strength to you.

To my sister Sandra and her family who welcomed me back home and continue to wrap their arms around me.

CONTENTS

FOREWORD

All My Springs: Journey of A Lifetime

The first time I read Carol's work, I was struck by the clarity of her voice, her sensitivity, and her ability to seamlessly weave history into a compelling emotional story about a devastating current event. I wasn't the only one moved by "Katrina: The Ghosts of 1865," her award-winning essay about social upheaval and personal loss in the wake of Hurricane Katrina.

Encouraged by her writing instructor, she wrote two other stories which also appeared in *Second Spring: An Anthology of Creative Writing by Seniors* in 2007—"Memories of Janet" and "The Calendar." They also appear in this volume. On numerous occasions during the two decades since our acquaintance, Carol talked about writing her own "strange and unexpected" life journey, but always seemed to be moving at warp speed with her travels, her fundraising ventures, her volunteerism, her maternal obligations and social activities, that is until she returned to her native Indiana, where she founded and currently facilitates the weekly Nora Commons

Creative Writing Workshop for members of her senior retirement community.

While I'm hard pressed to recall the specifics of our initial meeting as members of the Mills College community, I remember being taken by the energy, wit and compassion of this active "resumer," an older nontraditional student who'd lived in England as a young military wife and mother. "In the Little House in the Cul de Sac," she writes about motherhood and her fears for her infant son whose journey into manhood has become an unfathomable reality. A full-time Mills employee, and part-time degree student when we first met, Carol also worked as a weekend caregiver to a disabled young woman, whom she writes about in the touching story "Memories of Janet."

After earning her bachelor's degree in sociology, Carol summarily retired from college life, embarking upon a new profession as a certified substance abuse counselor for a women's residential drug program, where she honed her fund-raising skills as the nonprofit's development associate. Tired of hearing Oakland, her beloved second home for 36 years, constantly maligned, Carol launched a one-woman public relations campaign—an award-winning fundraising calendar highlighting the successes of the city's youth—which she recalls in "The Calendar."

In *All My Springs* she shares her "memories of a lifetime" in 28 stories, poems and personal essays. These gentle reflections of growing older and wiser with grace and passion provide a glimpse into how she's navigated the vicissitudes of a lifetime of springs. Whether writing about social ills in "Katrina: The Ghosts of 1865," heartbreak in "The Roses: A Garden of Secrets," a daughter's love in "Mama Won't You Play for Me Just One More Time?," traveling to the forbidden country of her dreams in "Discovering Life in Cuba," or childhood mischief during summers at Lake Maxinkuckee in "203 Hawkins Street," her writing is imbued with wisdom, longing, love, dignity, and good old mother wit.

For years, I've been encouraging Carol to tell her stories. I'm glad she'd slowed down long enough to write a few of them down and share them with you in this volume.

Best read with a heart open wide, just as they were written.

Enjoy!

Arabella Grayson
Writer/Curator
Two Hundred Years of Black Paper Dolls

INTRODUCTION

If memories can no longer live in our minds, then where can they live? Where they have lived for centuries: inside volumes of books. Your written words can live long after you. Generation after generation.

I want memories of my life to live in the hearts and minds of my family and friends. I watched a friend's precious life memories silenced forever when she took her last breath. She wanted so much to write them down for her family, but her time ran out. We can't depend on others to be the stewards of our memories.

For me, writing is cathartic and an educational exercise. For my reader, I want my stories to provoke, engage and inspire. If you are expecting them to all have happy endings, then many would be fiction. My stories are my journey through life, sometimes depicting great adversity and pain.

I once heard a Sunday sermon about retelling family stories. The minister said that we always tell the stories that are humorous and happy, never wanting to repeat the ones that are sad, embarrassing, or frightening.

"In the Bible, the first story book, all stories are not happy ones. Your Cain and Abel stories should also be told. We don't know, when telling such stories, if they can be a source of healing for those in pain," the minister said.

There is only one fiction story in my book—"The Traveling Heart." The story idea is based (in part) on a true event. I always considered writing fiction a waste of my time—I have too many nonfiction stories to tell and so little time to tell them.

In 2009, I started a creative writing workshop in my senior residential community. I always try and encourage other seniors to start thinking about a written legacy. You are never too old to learn new ways and continue growing—making a difference in your life and others, and keeping the past in the present. When I embarked upon this path of my life's journey, I had very little concern about being stricken by a memory problem, other than the normal loss that comes with aging. Nevertheless, I enrolled in an Alzheimer's clinical research study for two years.

Every sixty-nine seconds in the United States someone is diagnosed with Alzheimer's, and at this time, there is no cure for the disease. It crosses all ethnicities, races and genders. While in this study for seniors, I was the recipient of so many new research methods now used by scientist and doctors, who are on the brink of discovering and uncovering the mysteries of Alzheimer's. During that experience, I thought more and more about the importance of protecting my memories. I've known for a very long time that I wanted to write, but now the reason for writing was never more apparent.

I believe it is important to think of our legacies in terms other than monetary. My written legacy, as recorded in my book, is a compilation of short stories, poems and personal essays.

We must become the "legacy keepers."

ACKNOWLEDGMENTS

I am indebted to so many friends and associates who have contributed to my "learning tree." The members of the East Oakland Creative Writing Workshop truly enjoyed learning from each other, and they continue to thrive and flourish in the richness of their literary art. We received excellent training from our instructor Jennifer King and her team. Thanks, Jennifer, for teaching me to trust my own words, and just let them flow with feeling and description. And I learned from you that words don't always flow perfectly the first time and that the eternal critic inside of me just needs to calm down.

Of course, I am forever grateful to the Nora Commons Creative Writing Workshop. My feelings are expressed in the magazine article that appears in this book. This shared learning experience is invaluable to me. I am most grateful to Holly Powell, who was extremely helpful and supportive whenever I needed her. She was always available to listen and then give her expert advice.

From the West Coast to the Middle West, another friendship has remained spiritually strong, ripe with realism, and pleasantly content. This friend who has been in my life for a very long time, and has repeatedly been there to throw out the lifeline and save me—my heartfelt love and a lifetime of appreciation to Arabella Grayson for her eternal belief in me, and especially for her editing support that assisted in creating my written legacy. I thank you.

During my fundraising days in Oakland, I had nothing but high praise and appreciation for everyone's support and hard work that helped bring to fruition Oakland's first calendar (Positive Images of Oakland) recognizing and honoring our youth. It was the beginning of my love for the art of writing.

Then there were the ladies I counseled at *The Solid Foundation Mandela House Programs,* who taught me more than I could have ever taught them about courage and survival. And the founder and executive director Minnie Thomas, who trusted in me and believed that I could deliver on my promises to her—thank you.

After "seventy-four springs," I say thank you to all the generous and loving people who touched my life and helped me to survive "All My Springs."

RETURNING HOME
ON THE CALIFORNIA ZEPHYR

My last days in California were spent at a friend's home, sharing memories and coming to the realization that we would be living thousands of miles apart. That evening, she hosted a lovely party for me and many of our friends to say goodbyes. (Many of those guests had attended another party given for me two weeks earlier by another long-time friend.)

The following morning, my friend drove me to the train station. We hugged and shared expressions of "best wishes" for our futures. Because of her insatiable spirit of adventure, we had traveled the world. I learned how fascinating, old and beautiful our world is, thanks to her. This friend turned what could have been an untraveled existence into a life of adventure and learning, which continues to this day. We now take shorter trips and stay closer or within the U.S.

I went inside the train station to complete my final ticket arrangements. I found a seat and waited for the arrival of the *California Zephyr*. After 36 years, I was returning to where I call home. Even after all the years in California, it was never like home—especially in the fall and at Christmas.

I had packed two journals for this trip to make sure thoughts and feelings would be recorded. Memories of my years in California with family and friends were important to me. But getting to know all the "greats"—nieces and nephews—in my sister's family, continuing my writing, and growing old gracefully, was now my paramount goal.

Before long, I heard my train announcement. I collected all my belongings, stepped outside on this heavenly day and started walking next to the tracks—watching my train approach. I listened to the familiar rumbling and screeching sound of steel on the tracks and that famous whistle announcing its arrival.

My heart beat with excitement about the prospect of returning to my roots and starting a new life. After all those years, I knew I just couldn't pick up where my life had left off. So many of my friends were deceased and others had evolved into people I hardly recognized as once being my friends. We were no longer children and had traveled different life journeys. But I knew I could settle down and just start doing whatever I needed to do without any fear.

After my train stopped, a line began to form. I overheard someone say, "This line is for first-class passengers." I was grateful to have received the gift of a first-class ticket for my return home. I watched a train attendant approach us, calling my name. I was startled, but quickly composed myself and held up my hand. "Please come with me," she said. "My name is Kathy. I will be your attendant, all the way to Chicago." Then, reaching for my luggage, she led the way to the next train car.

She was a tall, big-boned woman, with short blond hair poking out from underneath her blue train cap. She wore a dark blue uniform over a starched white blouse, with a small blue tie. As I ascended the train steps, she talked about her responsibilities and my location on the train.

After entering my compartment, she showed me how the sofa turned into a bed. (There was also an overhead bed.) She would check with me in the evenings and mornings—just buzz her when I wanted my bed made. She continued showing me where things were and how to use different gadgets that would make my life comfortable for the next three days.

There was an armchair, a small table that hung from the wall, or could be pushed up when not in use, a full-length mirror, and my toilet and shower. There was a small sink with a mirror above, and cabinet space underneath that held extra towels. I also had a small closet with three hangers. She showed me where the coffee, tea, juices, and rolls were, near my compartment.

Carol returning to Indianapolis on the California Zephyr, April 2007.

I was given the hours for service in the diner and information about other train amenities. The attendant excused herself and closed my door.

After becoming familiar with my surroundings and finding convenient places for my belongings, I discovered the great view from a large window in my compartment. If I left the curtain in front of my door pulled back, I could see through the windows directly across the aisle. I didn't want to miss the picture—perfect views of the San Francisco skyline, the Golden Gate Bridge, and the imposing view of the Bay.

The observation cars have glass bubble roofs that give a panoramic view of the mountains. They offer a chance to meet and talk with other travelers. The seats are designed to swivel and show a full view from any position. There are tables nearby for refreshments. The first night I retired early—too much excitement!

The next morning I had breakfast brought to my compartment. I might as well test the service! I was excited about my first full day on the train. I loved walking through the train cars, rocking side to side, and taking cautious steps to balance myself while pushing open the sliding doors between the cars, then walking past the many riders, on my way to the dining car for my lunch. I always loved going there for meals. The first things to notice were tables along both sides of the train car, covered with white table cloths and floral center pieces on each table. Diners were met at the door by the attendant. "Good afternoon, Madam. How many, please?" I answered, "Good afternoon, one, please." The attendant led me to a table, helped me with my chair, handed me a menu and said "Your waiter will be right here." I responded with a smile. The view was perfect from any table and the service and food was good.

For the rest of my trip, I kept occupied in and out of my compartment, enjoying and exploring my surroundings, speaking to travelers, calling my friends and family with updates on my whereabouts, writing "thank-you" notes for gifts and heartfelt words from all the friends who had attended the parties given for me. I was coming home with lots of optimism about my future.

I looked out my window at the rear of the train, slowly curving around the tracks and climbing past huge rocks. I went to the observation car to witness nature; we were in Colorado. The scenery was magnificent as we followed the Colorado River. Suddenly there were mountains resembling red clay, with greenery protruding through. Sandy dry spots appeared and disappeared into the Colorado River. Clear, quiet water slowly rippled over rocks, in deep gorges. Nature is a perfect landscaper.

Our first stop, where we disembarked and made some purchases, was at Grand Junction, Colorado. The mountain air was wonderful! We did a little shopping at the general store, and then continued on our way to Chicago. We were running eight hours behind. Once we left Colorado our train was able to make up some of the lost time.

California Zephyr

Back in my compartment, I stared out the window and my mind drifted back to my first plan for retirement. It wasn't the "coming-home plan." I thought about how close I had come to living out my dream to live in Mexico, in an American retirement community. I remembered the first time I ever laid eyes on that place. I never imagined such a piece of paradise existed within my reach.

That was going to be my paradise on earth, hidden away from everything I wanted to leave behind. I just wanted to be left alone to reach the end of my journey, in peace. That beautiful place between the majestic red clay mountains and the Sea of Cortez, about three hours from San Diego, would bring the peace of mind and serenity to my soul that I so badly sought.

I purchased a lovely corner lot with flowering cactus plants that would surround the house I would build. I paid faithfully on my land with dreams of a brightly-colored stucco house, with a veranda, beautifully tiled floors, tiled walls in the kitchen and bathrooms. The house would have lots of windows and open spaces with views of the majestic mountains and hundreds of blooming and flowering cactus plants. This was going to be my retirement dream—come true.

The community around my land was a bustling, growing place with many American families living out their dreams. How I envied them—this was what I also wanted. I wanted to live among all this beauty, peace, wonderful amenities and resources this American retirement community would provide. The white sandy beaches, with many water sports, restaurants, a spa, golf course, exercise facilities and much, much, more. This was all next to a tiny, sleepy Mexican town with lots of shops and restaurants. Also, a small well-equipped hospital and clinic was nearby. But the downturn in the California housing market foiled my dream.

I picked up my journal and started to write down my memories. That's all I had left of my paradise. Now I'm going farther away than I ever thought I would be from my paradise—traveling east. Is there another plan I know nothing about?

That night, I was awakened by the roar of the engines, the train whistle, and the side-to-side rocking from the speed of the train. We were out of the mountains. I didn't sleep well that night. I kept peeping out my window, admiring the star-filled sky and trying to recognize images from the light of a full moon. I didn't regret choosing the train over the airplane. I accomplished much. I had time to think and contemplate what I wanted to put on my "bucket list."

The next morning I awakened to gaze at cornfields, John Deere billboards, white farm houses, red barns, silos and grazing cows. What a difference a few days make! Tonight we would arrive in Chicago, only six hours late, and missing my connection. I will be a little sad to leave the train and all the wonderful memories. I was remembering the friendly lady from Utah I met and invited to visit with me in my compartment. She was traveling for the first time on a train and had not been in the compartments. There was also that good-looking young couple from Florida I met in the upper lounge and had drinks with, while we tried to solve all the problems of the world.

It was time to start tiding up things and organizing my packing. Soon the attendant came to my compartment announcing our arrival. Late that night, I disembarked from the train and had to be rushed, by one of the station attendants, to my bus. After a four-hour bus ride from Chicago I arrived safely in Indianapolis at 3:00 a.m. I was very tired, but delighted to be greeted lovingly by my very sleepy and smiling sister. She had come alone. The marching band and the "Welcome Back Home" signs had not arrived!

MISS LEONA AND
THE CAREGIVER

O *ur lives time and again take strange and unexpected paths. We become "a test of the times." We often open our arms and our hearts to others, not knowing what we will give or give up in the end. Sometimes repayment comes in ways we would never imagine, but if it doesn't there are no regrets.*

After my glorious trip home to Indianapolis on the California Zephyr, I settled in at my sister's comfortable, eight-year-old home in the landmark Fort Harrison district. It was so nice to be at home with my family. Spring was arriving and my sister's lovely flower garden would soon be in full bloom. She always planted tulips, daffodils, hyacinths, roses, azaleas, heath and camellias. I could learn a few things about gardening from her.

Shortly after arriving, I submitted papers for a part-time substitute position in the public schools. While I was waiting to hear about employment, I spent my days making phone calls to family and old friends. I then remembered I hadn't phoned Leona, my step mother-in-law, who was now ninety-two. In 1995 I had married Leona's stepson (now deceased).

Leona was widowed for many years and never had children. I always called or visited with her whenever I was in Indianapolis. She was doing well for her age, but I often worried about how much longer she could handle her affairs, especially after I had observed piles of personal papers on her dining room table the last time I visited. Once her health started failing, who was going to be there for her? I had never met any of her close relatives. The niece and two nephews I heard her speak of lived out of state, or in another town. Her cousins in Indianapolis didn't seem to come around that much.

It was her church home of over 50 years that she often spoke about. She always mentioned how friends came from her church to visit and bring special gifts during the holidays. This revelation told me how very alone she was. I was impressed by her bravery and strength, and I admired her tenacity.

My call to her found the same delightful Leona with a voice full of joy and surprise to hear from me. I reminded her of the reason I returned, and that I no longer lived in California. She was pleased and wanted to know when she would see me.

In a few weeks, I called again and learned Leona had suddenly moved. "Oh, I moved," she timidly said. I was bowled over and confused. I said, "Leona—moved where?" *How could a 92-years-old lady move after 25 years or more in her home? What could have happened, I thought?* She said, "I moved to the Miller Mason Apartments," and then she gave me the address.

If my memory is correct, this old place was there when I was a child. The square-shaped building of red brick and old-style small-frame windows was certainly a relic from the past. In my opinion, this place was not suitable for an elderly lady of 92 years old. The building was just a few blocks from her old house, on a very busy street, in a neighborhood known to be unsafe.

When I inquired about why she had moved so suddenly and how she had managed to do so, she told me that the bank was selling her house and neighbors had helped her move. As I continued to ask more and more questions, she became embarrassed and unwilling to continue talking about her situation. Poor Leona must have gone through a terrible ordeal, so I decided to visit her as soon as possible and not ask any more questions. I assured her I would see her soon.

The next day, with great anticipation about what I would discover, I drove over to visit with Leona. How well I remembered that old building from my childhood. As I drove up, I noticed how red and fresh the brick appeared to be—probably from a recent water blasting. A large sign hanging over the front entrance invited new renters, saying, "Newly Remodeled—First Month Free."

With my heart pounding loudly, and sad thoughts of what I would discover, I parked near the entrance and proceeded up to the door. I couldn't ring the door bell for her unit because there was an empty hole where the door bell belonged.

As I searched for my cell phone, I thought about what else I would find missing inside. She answered my call with her usual jovial voice and informed me she would walk downstairs and let me in—there was no elevator. I thought about how difficult it must be for this 92-year-old woman, coming down two flights of stairs, to let me in and then going back up those two flights. Then I heard her struggling to open the large, heavy door. She greeted me with her usual life-size hug.

As I followed her up the stairs, I noticed her firm step, perfectly balanced with healthy looking legs—not hesitating for a moment. Leona was always dressed in something tasteful and comfortable. For years she had worn a short, brownish-red wig which complemented her fair skin. Once when I was visiting her, she had suddenly pulled it off and showed her silver-grey, baby-fine hair, that barely covered her scalp. Just as quickly as she had removed the wig, she smashed it back on. In her youth she had been a very attractive lady, and at 92 she remained youthful because of her petite figure.

We continued down a drab, dimly-lit hall with thin brown carpet and freshly-painted tan walls. When she reached her apartment, I stood quietly behind her, waiting to enter. She had been here for about three months. She said to me with a wave of her hand, "Come in and have a seat."

I was horrified by what I saw. I didn't know where I wanted to sit—it was just that uninviting; things looked clean, but just so much clutter and a strange furniture arrangement. I had always found her home neat and clean, with an inviting and comfortable seating arrangement. I felt sad as she directed me to a small flowered chair with tattered upholstery. Next to it was an old end table and lamp with a worn shade. She sat in a large brown leather chair, not in any better condition. There was a broken TV sitting in the middle of the floor, in front of a drop-leaf table. Above the table were windows with the air conditioner hanging from the ledge. Her bed was in the small dining area next to the tiny turnaround kitchen. There was absolutely nothing I could recognize from her house of 25 years.

I tried to relax enough to start a conversation, but I could only think of question after question. Where could I start, so I asked, "Why did this happen to you and how did you get here? What happened to all your furniture?" She started telling me about the bank taking the house she and her husband had rented all those years.

"Rented!" I exclaimed.

"My neighbors helped me move, and they had to set a lot of my furniture outside in front of my garage," she heartbreakingly said.

I just sat quietly and then I said, "I'm so sorry this had to happen to you, Leona. Is there anything I can do to help you?"

"Thank you," she said. Then she asked, "Could you come over and help me wash clothes in the basement of the building?"

"Yes I will Leona. When do you need me to come?" I also offered to take her to the grocery store whenever she wanted to go.

I couldn't shake the feeling that there was something on the horizon for me that would require my full attention. Little did I know how much my world would be altered with the simple reality that helping another human being could not be disregarded; therefore, I must have a plan on how I can help Leona without her feeling I am intruding in her life.

"If you could come over later this week and help me wash would be just fine," she said.

"Sure Leona. Just tell me what day this week and the time you want me to come."

I thought to myself: *When we get this task out of the way, we will need to get down to some really serious business, since it seems like I'm the only one she can depend on.*

She decided that the next day would be just fine for us to do laundry. I told her I would come over the next morning around ten o'clock. I lived about ten miles away. On the way over I would stop and pick up a clothes basket and washing powder.

I had never seen the basement where the laundry room was located. After walking through two long, dimly-lit corridors resembling the ancient tombs of the Pharaohs without hieroglyphics, I felt buried, but just not dead; that was really a scary feeling. Then I discovered she didn't have enough quarters for the machines. I had no choice but to leave Leona in that creepy, tomb-like place until I returned with quarters, since we had already started washing her clothes. I left with instructions for her not to move and I promised it wouldn't take long for me to walk down the street to the bank. Not letting anyone see me driving away would be a good idea. Some of the residents in her building appeared to be unemployed and unemployable, for one reason or another.

When I returned from my sprint to and from the bank, I was happy and relieved to find Leona quietly sitting by the washing machines, unharmed and excited about telling me how she had removed the first load of clothes from the washer and put them in the dryer. It frightened me to leave her alone; I wanted to get out of that dungeon and go home to try and to contemplate what my next move would be in this lady's life. I needed to get as much information about her life and family as possible. I also wanted to email her stepdaughter in California, my sister-in-law, explaining what I had discovered. While living in California, we had often spoken of Leona and our concerns for her well-being. My sister-in-law was frightened of traveling, so that was one of the reasons I always stayed in contact with Leona and visited with her whenever I was in Indianapolis.

When I contacted her stepdaughter with the grim news of her living arrangements, I was blunt and candid about what I had discovered and how I could be of assistance, but that the range of my assistance was limited. What needed to be done was to first find her a proper place to live as quickly as possible, but I had no control over that without knowing about her financial situation. She had refused to contact any of her relatives for this discussion and made a remark about maybe just turning everything over to me.

I bought myself a small journal to keep track of any important information for future reference. I had her give me her Social Security number, date of birth, place of birth, doctor's name, medications and her deceased husband's information, in case any emergencies would occur. Leona was very cooperative and seemed to enjoy the fact I was serious about assisting her.

That evening in my bedroom, I took a rare moment to think about my trip home on the California Zephyr. I carefully contemplated my future life. I made my "bucket list" and was determined to stick with it. It didn't seem too important anymore. Life has a way of getting in the way of things, and in this case it was someone else's life. On that train I had felt so reassured and resolute in all things pertaining to my future, because if I hadn't, I would have been easily bloodied by my life's disappointments and pains. It had taken me years to reach for and build such bold confidence and feelings of worthiness.

The phone rang and it was Leona's step-grandson in Louisiana, who sounded concerned and worried about the only grandmother he knew well during his childhood. His father's mother died when he was a very young child. Leona was the grandmother who was always around for his children, and they often made trips to visit her or vise versa. He immediately asked me to take care of everything I could, to please keep him informed of our progress, and that money was on the way to assist in getting her moved to a senior community. How grateful I was to have his help. I certainly needed a partner.

The most daunting thing I had to do was approach Leona about moving again—so soon. I wasn't sure how all this would affect her, since she believed where she now lived was just fine. I had to find a way to remove Leona from her predicament and hopefully change her feelings.

I asked for assistance from my sister, since I didn't know much about the city. I wanted to take a very gentle approach with Leona and do my best to convince her she needed to be somewhere more suited to her needs. It would probably be a better approach if I could identify a few places, visit them and then bring her back to see them.

I remember years ago asking Leona if she had ever considered moving into a senior community. She looked very baffled and shook her head, "no." Later I realized she didn't understand what a senior community was. She was not aware of her choices for comfort and convenience.

One day I was in her apartment when there was a knock at the door. When she asked who it was, a lady responded with a request to use her phone. I told Leona not to open the door and to tell her no. The lady went away and I started questioning her about who she was, but she couldn't remember her name and just said she was a lady who lived in the building. This frightened me and I told her never let anyone in who wasn't family or a friend. I pleaded with her to promise me she would never let this lady in again to use her phone. The next day Leona told me the lady came back and knocked on her door several times. I could tell she was disturbed by this relentless knocking at her door.

That night I didn't sleep well thinking about how Leona could be a target for some criminal activity. I decided to make a sign and put on her door. The sign read:

"Please do not disturb this resident requesting to use her phone. If you continue knocking on her door, the

police will be called. This problem was reported to the Manager's Office. Thank you."

The next day the sign had been taken down. I'm sure it was the lady wanting to use the phone. Right then I made up my mind to hurry and start this home search for Leona. I decided to take her to the senior community I believed to be the best fit. I was so nervous about what her reactions would be.

It was a warm summer day and I was feeling optimistic about Leona's future when I decided this would be the day I would take her to American Village for a tour and have a discussion about the possibility of living in that facility. I hoped to convince her that change can be pleasant and exciting, even at her age. She had kept very quiet about any move and she never let on whether she would or would not consider it. I still had no idea about income, but I remained unrelenting and pushed on. I had even contacted a friend with a truck who would move her things, at a moment's notice, to the new location. It would not be a difficult move because I would only take the furniture that was in fairly good condition; the balance would be taken away by the Salvation Army.

Leona remained very quiet and never asked any questions. I had no clue what she must have been thinking. As we drove up to the front of the attractive building with lovely landscaping, I was recalling how impressed I was with the tour my sister and I had taken a few days before. The main lobby of the building was attractively decorated with wallpaper, art, flowers, plush carpeting, and turn-of-the-century furniture. The apartments on the second level left me with a good feeling about Leona's comfort, if this plan could come to fruition.

When we entered the building we were greeted by the receptionist. I gave her our names, and she proceeded to call the guide and interviewer. Leona had remained very quiet, taking it all in. Her eyes darted back and forth with a look of excitement, telling me she was pleased with what she saw. But what she heard was processed with caution and skepticism. I watched an expression of consternation follow us all through our tour. A shadow of doubt walked between us.

Leona's hands tightly gripping her purse told me she was nervous about the cost. She did not know about the financial help coming from her step-grandson. I had no idea how she would feel about his help. I didn't think it was time to share this information with her.

Our discussion with the staff person regarding the business issue was limited and unintentionally shallow, because I knew so little about Leona's finances. We did not have time for her to see the garden homes. I believed they were not suited for her because they were a little isolated. On the way home she hardly talked and neither did I, except to say we both agreed the surroundings and the people were warm and friendly. We both felt the strain of all this uncertainty, and I am sure she was once again experiencing feelings of disorder in her life.

Once we returned to Leona's apartment, I helped her with dinner.

She suddenly asked, "Carol, would you take me to the bank tomorrow? My personal banker needs to meet with me. I missed going last week because I had no one to take me." I thought, *What could this be all about?* I assured her I would.

That night at my sister's home I sat and contemplated what my experience might be, and why she had this important meeting. I assured my sister that I would only be "driving Miss Daisy." I just hoped everything would go smoothly for her.

The next day, while driving Leona to the bank, we rode in silence. I was heavy in thought about what this meeting was all about. I felt a little anxious being drawn more and more into her life, and having to put my own life on hold. I could hardly think about anything else except how this was all going to end.

I totally forgot that I was waiting to hear from the Indianapolis Public Schools about my application for substitute teaching. I wanted just a couple of days' work each week in my retirement years. I was just picking up the fragments of my life and trying to create some sense of order and purpose.

When we pulled up in the parking lot of the bank, she asked, "Will you go in with me?" "Yes, I will, Leona," I responded.

Once inside we sat on chairs in the area of the tellers' windows. Leona was invited by a bank official to come into her office. I sat trying to read a magazine, only to experience racing thoughts about what was going on in that office. Several times I heard the banker's voice saying that she must get her affairs in order.

What did this mean? I decided that whenever I could speak to the banker, I wanted her to have my contact information in case Leona couldn't be reached.

Shortly after that thought, the door to the office opened and there stood the banker saying, "Ms. Conley, I will be talking with you in just one moment." I shook my head and smiled. Then I became a little nervous about what she wanted with me. This was the first time I believed, just maybe, someone in Indianapolis could convince Leona to listen to what I thought was necessary and crucial for her welfare. I sat tapping my foot, squirming around in my chair and breathing deeply while I waited for the office door to open again.

Leona had been born just one year before my deceased mother. Good old mom couldn't be here, but she was making sure her daughter kept up her altruistic obligations.

Okay Mama, this is for you.

"Ms. Conley, could you come in, please," the bank officer said.

"Yes, thank you," I said. I rose nervously with stiff, quick steps and walked past her, into the office. Leona turned, her eyes following me to the chair next to her.

"Have a seat, Ms. Conley. I was just talking with your mother-in-law about her financial affairs," said the banker. She was a young Black woman with professional demeanor and a pleasant smile, whose patience must have held up magnificently with Leona over the years. Leona had spoken kindly of her on our way to the bank.

I noticed a pile of mail on the bank officer's desk which belonged to Leona. I had always wondered who helped Leona with the mail after spotting stacks of it in recent years on her dining room table. *So, this is where she would bring her mail—to this lady.* The banker mentioned how this could not be her responsibility because it was against bank policies. It just wasn't legal.

I sat nervously biting my lips and squeezing my hands as the conversation soon advanced to the banker asking my mother-in-law if she would allow me to handle her affairs. She also said that she needed to give me a Power of Attorney in order to make this happen.

The banker then said, "Mrs. Conley, do you understand why you must have help with your business affairs?" Leona responded by nodding her head "yes." Then the banker turned to me and asked if I would be willing to take on this responsibility. There was a moment of silence then I answered, "Only if there would be no interference from any of Leona's relatives." I was assured by the bank officer there wouldn't be and I must remain in control.

Leona sat quietly next to me with her hands folded around her purse. As I looked at her, I tried to read her thoughts, but her facial expression remained stoic and her eyes stared down at the papers. The bank officer put a form in front of her and gave her a pen to sign her name.

Then an official-looking form and a pen were pushed in front of me for my personal information and signature. What was I agreeing too? Responsibility for someone's life was no small matter. My hand felt sweaty and my stomach was in knots. Everything was happening so quickly.

After we finished, the banker commenced to move her computer monitor closer for me to see. I was looking at Leona's bank statement. I thought about how frugal she was; denying her self the very basics of life, living in the most austere manner, when there was no need for that. Her deceased husband had provided her with a modest inheritance that would hopefully last her for the rest of her life.

I recalled, having read an article about "How to Tell Who Lived During the Depression." It said how you can always tell Depression survivors by what they save. Leona saved all the things this article mentioned: paper bags, bottles and jars, all sizes of plastic containers, strings, rubber bands, twist ties, bread bags, and all food.

I sat there in the bank realizing how much easier it all was going to be. Now I would move forward with plans to get her relocated to a safer place. But that just may be easier said than done with her passive/aggressive personality.

We left the bank in silence, carrying the newly-signed papers giving me authority over every aspect of Leona's life.

I didn't know what to say to her. Thank you certainly didn't seem appropriate. Did I dare ask her how she felt about her life being handed over to me, a person she only knew as her daughter-in-law, who always had lived thousands of miles away? Where could I start with my long list of concerns for Leona? For now, I just wanted to go home and try and comprehend what this all meant, assure her everything would be all right, and get a good night's rest to start out fresh in the morning.

The next morning I put my very important piece of paper away in a safe place after making copies. Then I phoned Leona to start making plans for the next few days. I received all the money necessary from her step-grandson to pay for our upfront expenses for American Village. Important decisions would have to be made by her and myself very soon.

The next day I picked up Leona and took her to American Village Senior Community where I showed her the lovely garden homes. After much thought, I had decided we could live together. We would have a little house with a screened porch, garden and a view of the lake from the kitchen window. I prayed she would perhaps see the many benefits and comforts available to her and begin to accept and rejoice in the fact she would soon be moving to a much nicer place. Her reactions were mute with a forced smile as she walked through every room.

One evening at my sister's home I shared my thoughts about moving in with Leona. This would certainly make my life easier when I thought about all the trips I would otherwise make to Leona's apartment. What would I do in the middle of the winter? My sister wasn't too thrilled about this idea. She thought I was giving up too much and would regret my decision, but I was determined to push on with this plan. I convinced her that I would make this work.

I spent one day taking inventory of the items in her apartment. Some things we could keep and everything else would be given to the Salvation Army. I purchased boxes and we started wrapping and packing dishes and other glass items. I hired my two great nieces to help, since they were out of school for the summer and could use the extra money.

Leona remained very quiet and hardly asked any questions. I kept reassuring her everything would be all right. Soon, she seemed to trust me and was very cooperative. I was determined to do what I thought needed to be done for her life. She jumped right in and helped pack.

I broke the news to Leona about the both of us moving into the nice garden home in a senior community because it just made sense and would accommodate my life style, since I was also a senior needing some of the same resources. Through her tightly-closed lips she forced a smile while her hazel eyes remained large and sad.

"Please trust me, life will be so much nicer for you," I said.

"Yes," she said and continued wrapping her dishes to be placed in the packing box.

I had made arrangements for my household items and hers to be picked up on the same morning, and then I would take her directly to the new place. I would return to her apartment later in the week to meet the Salvation Army. I wanted her to be moved and never have to come back to the apartment and see what was being given away.

Once at the new place, the first thing to do was to get her bedroom and mine in order. I could manage the kitchen with the help of my great-nieces. When we arrived at the house, I watched Leona walk from room to room with a look of consternation. She was not so sure about this place. She had been just fine where she was. I took her to the screened porch and showed her how charming and comfortable it could be in the summer. We just needed to plant flowers and purchase porch furniture. How wonderful it would be to sit there and look up at the stars and the moon on those warm summer nights.

During the 25 years she had lived in her tiny home, she had never had a porch to sit on or a garden to enjoy. The outdoors was not a part of her life, except for leaving and returning from her garage to the house. Once inside, the door slammed and the deadbolt and chains went "clank." The one exception from the mundane was her church affiliation of 50 years and her membership and participation in the National Council of Negro Women for more than 40 years.

I remember the day I found her collection of awards and recognitions carefully placed in a scrapbook. I took them to her and sat next to her on the sofa. We both looked through her book and she smiled with her heart full of memories. She had stayed very busy working and traveling with the National Council of Negro Women.

The morning finally arrived for the movers. My plan for arriving in Indianapolis to retire and be with the family seemed years behind me, and my life now filled with so many new experiences and responsibilities—way more than I had bargained for. However, I'm sure Leona might have felt she also was getting much more than she had bargained for.

The move went well, and so far all my plans where falling into place. After many trips to Wal-Mart, and making decisions about what pieces of furniture we would need to purchase to make the house comfortable, Leona was feeling more cheerful about her new surroundings and operating at her usual speed. I decided to gradually introduce her to all the new resources she would have. The first was just being able to have a place where she could take a walk without being afraid.

I had discovered that after Leona stopped driving, no one at her church seemed to notice she had not been attending. When I found out how she was being treated, I was furious. So I took her to church one Sunday to find out to whom I could speak about having her picked up and brought home every Sunday.

Looking forward to church again, Leona started preparing her clothes and bathing on Saturday night. Then on Sunday morning she looked elegant and attractive walking out the door. I would make sure there was a snack to carry in her purse because I couldn't get her to eat anything before leaving. I always prepared a scrumptious Sunday-afternoon meal that was ready for her when she returned.

Leona Conley

Then, starting on Mondays, I let her decide what activity she wanted to be a part of for that week. I encouraged her to try and get out at least twice a week. She enjoyed watching her TV programs during the day and sitting on the sun porch. She would spend hours there just watching and listening to the birds and reading her news papers and magazines. She seemed to be so content.

Every day I had to work my way through understanding all the business affairs she had not been able to handle, and try and take care of my own affairs. I had to resign from my part-time position at the schools. I found it too exhausting to get up so early in the mornings, and have the energy I needed to keep up with the children. So I became a full-time caregiver.

Friends often came to visit with Leona, and finally a cousin came. We had birthday parties, barbeques, and an ice-cream social in our spacious yard for all the children in my family. We celebrated Christmas with a tree on our screened porch, beautiful decorations and an old-fashioned dinner with all the trimmings the first Christmas we were there.

In the spring we planted flowers and tomatoes. Leona enjoyed watering the plants and she could hardly contain herself from picking the tomatoes before they were large enough. She seemed to be thrilled with her new life. This just reminded me that we are never too old to experience something for the first time.

She loved the outings on our shuttle bus, shopping during the day, events throughout the city, and sometimes evening trips to just sightsee. The evening trips were especially nice at Christmas time, looking at all the house decorations. I hoped this was a period of her life she would affectionately remember, instead of all the lonely and drab days when she could no longer have her outside activities. Then, too, maybe she didn't know anything about lonely and drab, but just accepted her life without any complaints or regrets. This could have just been my perception of her life and I hadn't saved her from something she hadn't accepted.

Life wasn't always perfect for Leona and me. Sometimes we would have our differences about how she wanted to handle her own business, without consulting me. Her greatest triumph was beating me to the mail box every morning. When she got the mail and opened it, I wouldn't know for sure if there was anything I also needed to respond to until I could convince her to let me see what she had gotten.

I would take her once or twice a month to the bank where she would draw out cash she needed for the month. She would buy what she wanted when I took her shopping at the store, and I would get the bulk of the food products we would need every week or two.

One day I asked Leona if she needed me to take her anywhere before I left for the day with my sister and some friends. She replied no because a lady friend from her church and Bible study group was coming to take her out for lunch. I learned later that she was one who picked Leona up and brought her home from Bible study every week.

When I returned home, Leona was unusually quiet. I asked if she had had a nice afternoon and she responded that she had. Soon after this I learned from a bank official that my name had been removed from Leona's account. She had come in to the bank with a friend who seemed to be warning her to never put anyone on her account. Needless to say, I was just livid and told the bank official that I would be bringing Leona in to get everything straightened out. It was close to the Thanksgiving holiday, so I decided to just let this go until after the first of the year. I wanted to have time to investigate this woman's behavior that day at the bank, and speak with a lawyer. I had transferred her account to a branch closer to her new residence, but I went back to the old bank and met with the lady I had first spoken with. We sorted through everything and she concluded this should never have happened.

The attorney drafted a letter for me, and after approving it, I asked him to mail the letter to Leona's church friend. The letter directed her to immediately cease and desist from any defamation of my character or she would be taken to court. Once the letter was sent I never heard or saw anything from her again, and she never picked Leona up again.

I showed Leona a copy of the letter from my attorney, but she never mentioned anything about it. Where was this devoted friend from her church when she couldn't get to services on Sunday, was my question. I eventually took Leona back to the bank and after having some very stern words for the banker, they explained to my mother-in-law why this was necessary, I was reinstated.

One day Leona came to me with her hands full of papers. I wondered what she had. Once she showed everything to me, I realized this was her way of saying to me, I think we had better start planning for my funeral. She had receipts and other confirmation for payment. Her husband had earlier prepaid for all funeral arrangements in Crown Hill Cemetery. I hadn't known how to initiate this subject, so she had done so in her quiet and graceful manner. That afternoon, after looking through everything, we decided when we would call Stuarts Mortuary for her appointment.

By the next couple of weeks, everything was arranged according to Leona's wishes. She had started her eulogy which I helped her complete by filling in dates, names of family members and her accomplishments. Leona knew many people and had been very active during her lifetime.

It was just in the last six or seven years that her activities had slowed and then ceased. This year she would be celebrating her ninety-third birthday.

I found a company which could send an attendant to check on Leona each day whenever I wanted to travel out of town with my family. I was comfortable with the lady because she worked for a family next door, and Leona also knew her. There were times when I just needed to get away. I think Leona probably needed to be away from me every once in a while also.

The next year was the first time I would see Leona ill. It was in the fall of the year, one Sunday, when she was dressing for church. She suddenly complained about feeling too warm. I was in my bedroom, reading the Sunday paper, when suddenly she called for me. Her voice sounded weak and alarming. She was sitting in her bedroom chair and had stopped dressing because she was having difficulty breathing. At her last medical appointment, nothing out of the ordinary had been reported by her heart specialist. Of course, at her age anything could happen. He had treated her for the last twelve years for heart congestion.

I immediately called 911 when I wasn't able to relieve her suffering. Hurriedly I dressed, while monitoring her condition and waiting anxiously for the ambulance. Once they arrived and administered oxygen, I answered questions as they prepared her to be transported to the hospital. I then jumped into my car and followed behind them, all the while in a state of disbelief how quickly this all happened. How do you prepare for this? You don't. I wanted to think I could protect her for a long time from any illnesses and have her around to still enjoy life.

When we arrived at the hospital, she was immediately taken into the emergency room where the doctor began examining her. She seemed to feel better and was resting well. I was still reeling with surprise and feeling a little shaky about how suddenly our peaceful Sunday morning had abruptly changed into this. So many questions in my head were drowning out any other sounds around me. The nurses and medical techs seemed only a blur, floating silently in and out of the room while I sat waiting in the chair at the foot of Leona's bed in the emergency wing.

Late that night Leona was released. It was storming outside when we left. The hospital attendants walked us to the door and remarked to us to be careful and get home safely. I remember how frightened I was driving through the heavy downpour, deafening thunder, and the lightning streaking through the sky. I never let on to Leona how nervous I was. Not much conversation took place between us. That night she appeared broken and shaky, and I was just too tired to say or do much else but make sure she was comfortable and ready for bed that night. Neither of us knew what to expect the next morning. After a good night's rest, I would try and see what plan I needed to put in place. The doctor had not prescribed any new medications. She had not had a heart attack, and no special instructions were given except to observe her closely and return if she showed any signs of her condition worsening.

Within a week Leona seemed comfortable with her life again: happy to return to Sunday church services, preparing her breakfast, back to enjoying TV, the sun porch, and the red-breasted robin that often landed in the tree near our porch. How short the sweetness was when there was another attack. For the next few weeks she was back and forth between her doctor and the emergency hospital room. Twice she was hospitalized for about a week. While in the hospital she would remove her intravenous tube, refuse to eat much of anything and suddenly developed a fear of her medication. She had always been so good about remembering to take it. She had been given another prescription that she said was making her sick. Now everything was moving in reverse and I was at the helm, just trying to keep going forward.

One of Leona's relatives who never bothered to talk with me (the niece in Michigan), suddenly started reaching out. This niece hadn't seen Leona in 15 or 20 years. When we moved, Leona had kept the same telephone number. The niece only started phoning regularly after she discovered I was in Leona's life and had moved her to a new home. I remember Leona looking at very old photographs, and I always wondered why she did not have any recent ones of family births, weddings and other events. Her relatives just hadn't bothered to stay in touch. She would pull out her photos of relatives and share them with me. She was proud of her family. The one thing I noticed about her family photos was how dated they all were. Nothing had been sent to her for many years of recent family events like births, weddings and other family events.

Because Leona was now unable to take care of many of her personal needs, I had hired a lady to be with her when I needed to be away. Our lives were now spinning out of control. She was getting weaker and weaker from not eating. I pleaded with her to eat, because if she didn't I wouldn't be able to keep her at home. She had even stopped talking. This was all so mysterious and disconcerting for me.

The last time Leona entered the hospital she never came back home. I had made arrangements to have her taken directly to a nursing home. This was heart-breaking because I knew she would never come out of there. She would lose hope and give up, just like my mom had. I worried about how she would be treated. But I knew if I visited with her almost every day her care would be better.

Once there, Leona just seemed to be defeated, but defiant and still not talking to anyone. She would sometimes grunt or make other strange sounds. She would scoot around in her wheel chair. She continued not to eat, so I would sit with her in the dining room trying to coax her to eat just a little. She was trying to tell everyone just to leave her alone because she had lived long enough. But we the living sometimes refuse to let go—for our own selfish reasons.

Leona started pulling her intravenous tube out of her arm again, and they would have to send her back to the hospital because none of their nurses were trained. I was disgusted and considered this to be weakness in their delivery services.

There were many disappointments and complaints I had about her care. She would constantly fall from her wheelchair until finally they tied her in. One day, when I went to visit, I found her lying on her mattress on the floor. I was told she would try to get up and then fall. I knew most of the staff was doing the best they could for her. They were all overworked and underpaid. I hoped she could just be at peace for whatever amount of time she had left.

I stayed busy looking after all her medical and personal details and trying to stay in touch with family and friends, who wanted to be kept informed about her health. Many of these same people had never spoken to me until they could no longer talk with Leona. One elderly friend was homebound and hadn't seen her for some time. Others had never or seldom been to visit her—some for years.

I will never forget the sudden request for Leona to attend an out-of-town family reunion shortly after we moved into American Village. It was one Friday afternoon and I had arranged for her to have a hearing test. While the hearing test was being done, her phone rang. Since she was not in her room, I answered. It was her cousin who was known to visit her once in a while. I introduced myself, and the reason the cousin gave for the call was to ask if Leona could be picked up and taken to a family reunion that afternoon. I explained what was taking place at that moment, so this wouldn't be a good time. She sounded quite disappointed, so I explained to her that I was responsible for Leona, and I would do what I thought was best.

I asked her cousin, when was the last time she attended? I was astonished to learn it had been seven years. So now what was the urgency? I politely told her Leona would not attend this year. Of course, I asked Leona if she wanted to go and she said she didn't think so. I'm sure these family members were interested in what was taking place in her life, after they did nothing to help her.

The back and forth to the hospital to replace intravenous needles continued for over a week. One day the hospital staff called me and said they wanted me to attend a meeting that coming Monday morning. This meeting was to discuss discontinuing replacing the intravenous needle in Leona's arm.

On Monday morning my phone rang about 8:00 a.m. When I answered, it was a staff person from the nursing home. She informed me that Leona was not doing well. Her feet were cold and she was unresponsive. She thought I should come right away. I started preparing to go when the phone rang again. This time it was to inform me she had passed.

I remembered sitting on the side of my bed, half-dressed and now in somewhat of a stupor thinking about my last visit with Leona. She had seemed to be very sad, her eyes absent of any hope. She was sitting tied in her wheel chair, but still trying to remove the intravenous tube from her arm. I took her hand and held it between my hands. I looked at her haggard face and hollow eyes, her frail and helpless body, while I struggled to find the right words to say to comfort her. Then tearfully I said, "Leona, it won't be much longer that you will have to suffer, and soon you will be with Mr. Conley again. Would you like that?" She slowly lifted her head, nodded, looked directly at me and smiled. I knew she was pleased and of all the promises I had made Leona, this was the one I surely needed the most help with.

After a difficult and frantic exit from the house, I drove to the nursing home and went directly to Leona's room. I saw her so at peace, and I felt relieved that my promise to her was delivered. I was a little sad that I had not been there to say my final goodbye. After a moment of silence I walked up to the nurse's desk and provided her with information she needed to release the body, and then the mortuary was called.

I remember thinking how Leona had taken matters in her own hands and decided not to wait for the Monday morning conference, therefore not burdening me with the difficult decision to let her die.

Surrounded by her lavender, the "great lady" had all her wishes granted for that day. Songs were dedicated, tributes given, and then goodbyes said: *Leona will always be remembered for her kind and gentle spirit. Her pleasant vitality was a continuous inspiration. We all appreciated the happiness she so willingly shared and inspired in her family and friends. When there is love, any life is too short.* (This appeared in her obituary).

I surely miss her—an awful lot. I learned so much about living so long and then dying with valor. I could never have known my true destiny on that train. Coming home was bringing me straight to her. I had to decide what was important in life and disregard all the other.

After Leona's death I found a photo identical to the one my mother always had that we were both in over 60 years ago. I later discovered she had also signed my sister's memorial book the day of her funeral in 1973. So this was proof of her past connections to my family and knowing my mother.

A young Leona and 9 year-old Carol.

203 HAWKINS STREET

*O*nce again I was on my way to spend the summer with my great aunt and uncle, who were childless and always looked forward to my visits. They lived in the town of Culver, Indiana. The bus ride from Indianapolis was not too long; I enjoyed the trip because I spent it dreaming about exciting, fun-time activities for the next six weeks of my summer. I always sat next to a window on the bus with my eyes gazing out at the countryside until I arrived and saw their smiling faces.

Mama had been sending me to Culver every summer since I was about eight years old, and this was my third trip. The bus ride went only as far as Plymouth and then my aunt and uncle would be there to pick me up and drive back to their home.

Their house was at the corner of Hawkins and Plymouth Streets, 203 Hawkins. I loved my stay there in their comfortable two-bedroom home, with its large living room and dining area. The kitchen was the place where so many good meals were prepared. My Uncle Jack spent a lot of time sitting on his screened-in porch, smoking his cigars. The porch was especially nice at night, protected from the bugs and cooled by the evening breeze. I had my own bedroom with the window next to the large old oak tree. There was always a cool breeze coming through my window at night.

From the kitchen I could look out the window and see beautiful Lake Maxinkuckee, where Uncle Jack's fishing boat was tied to the pier. Every day, white sailboats appeared along with one or two speedboats skillfully maneuvering across the lake with their *blaring motors, leaving behind miles of great white, double streams of waters.*

During the 1940s and '50s, this was a small community of middle-class Negroes who lived and worked in Culver—not known to many in Indiana. They had comfortable homes with screened porches and views of the lake. Many of the men worked at the military academy on the other side of the lake, where the wealthy families lived in large beautiful homes. My Uncle Jack had retired after 40 years in maintenance at the academy. He had earned a decent living and provided a comfortable home for Aunt Nell and himself.

Most whites were able to stay put in one place, earning a living, when too often Negroes were forced to move from one job to another, unable to accumulate much. But these folks in Culver had bought homes, sent their children to college and were now retired and living out their lives, enjoying small-town life.

Culver is famous for its military academy, founded in 1894 as the Culver Military Institute with 47 boys. Now the Culver Military Academy is coed. In 1957 two daughters of faculty and staff members enrolled and in 1959 the first two women received their diplomas. The campus of over 1800 acres lies on the north shore of Lake Maxinkuckee in northern Indiana. [1]

Shortly after returning to Indianapolis to retire, I saw an advertisement in the OASIS catalogue for a one-day trip to visit Culver and tour the military academy. What a thrill, and how exciting it would be to take this trip to my favorite

---

[1]   Website: Culver Academy Indiana

childhood place. I had never dreamed this would happen so soon because this place was certainly on my "bucket list." I wanted to return to recall the childhood memories of my Aunt Nell and Uncle Jack, and the house where they lived.

I made arrangements to go. We traveled by coach to Plymouth, just as I had as a little girl. Once we arrived in Plymouth, I remembered I would be in Culver shortly. Watching out the window, my memories traveled back to that time in my life. This was the closest to a time machine I would ever experience. I was again the little girl watching out the bus window for my aunt and uncle.

We first toured the military academy, the place from which Uncle Jack had retired. I never came here as a child. For the first time, I saw Culver's famous Black Horse Troupe close up. The horses were beautiful; we received instructions on their care and stroked their manes. Next we were taken to the chapel for a presentation and then to the school's beautiful library, built by the Huffingtons. It sat next to the lake with a magnificent view through a large glass wall. The stunning campus wound for miles around the lake. The students scurried back and forth across the campus with their books and other items. They were from all over the country and the world—ranging in age from 12 to 18.

I was excited and anxious to see the downtown area. I wondered how it would look after almost 60 years. We were to stop in town for lunch and then visit the shopping area. I had asked the tour guide if she was familiar with the neighborhoods, and she said no. But I was determined not to leave Culver until I knew whether or not the old family home was still there.

As we ate lunch I looked across the street at the entrance to the park where I used to play and take summer classes with my friend Thelma Lilly. Back on the street, I suddenly recognized the old movie theater. It was the only one in town and colored people were not allowed to attend. Since there were so many summer activities for children and my Uncle Jack always made sure I enjoyed myself, I didn't miss not going to the movie theater.

Our next stop was across from Main Street. Our tour guide announced we would only have about 30 minutes to visit the stores. As I looked up and down the street, nothing much seemed to have changed. I remember walking to town from my aunt and uncle's home. Oh, how I could feel the excitement building in my body! But I still did not remember where 203 Hawkins Street was. Suddenly I spotted a real estate office across the street from our bus. When people on the tour started to leave for the stores, I told my friends to go ahead and I would meet them back at the bus.

I knew that real estate office would be able to help me. When I opened the door, there was a lady sitting in front of her computer. She turned around and smiled, then asked, "Could I please help you?"

"Yes, please," I said. "Could you tell me where 203 Hawkins Street is?"

She asked me to wait just a moment while she pulled up some information on the computer. I could feel my adrenaline pumping faster and faster. I was ready to take off down some street, like a hound dog heading for his hunt, when the lady asked me to step up to the computer and showed me a street map.

"Not much has changed there. A few new houses have been built, and I bet you will find your home," she said. As I looked at the map I saw Hawkins Court instead of Hawkins Street. I guess that was called "progress." I had spotted new buildings around town. After getting directions, I thanked her and headed for the door and down to the corner to Main

Street. I was practically running because between sharing my childhood story and the computer search, I only had about 20 minutes before having to return to our coach. I bolted past store windows barely noticing the contents. Then I stopped to ask some workmen if I was heading in the right direction. "Yes," they said, "just turn left and head over to Plymouth Street, then turn right and you will be at the corner of Hawkins Court."

I was almost running down Plymouth Street in order to try and see as much as I could of my memories. Suddenly I recognized Thelma Lilly's house. It was closer to the lake than ours. I had never experienced such nostalgia—I was that little girl there again, hearing her friend's voice and running up and down the streets. Then I came to a corner where I just stood quietly for a moment, observing all the homes. Where was our home? I finally recognized it with a different front porch and a deck on the back. The wonderful screened porch where I spent so many warm evenings no longer was there. But there was my bedroom window near the large oak tree. All the other older homes were there, and two new homes.

When I crossed the street, walking slowly past the family home, I stood for just a moment as if to pay my respects to it. Then I started down the road that I traveled as a child, but suddenly I was stopped dead in my tracks, no longer able to reach the lake where Uncle Jack's boat stayed moored. It was now private property with lake-front homes. This was the reason the street was renamed "Hawkins Court."

I remembered Mrs. Williams' big white house on the corner. I could see her hanging large white sheets on the clothes line. Her house was directly across from ours. I stood remembering the day I found the snake under the dog house Uncle Jack built for his dog Peep. I screamed, ran inside the house, and brought my uncle outside to see it. He immediately killed the snake, and I watched with much curiosity while it wiggled until it died. Mrs. Williams had wanted to know what all the commotion was about. I yelled across the road that Uncle Jack had just killed a big snake. I asked her, "Do you want to see it?"

"Yes," she said. So I took the pitchfork Uncle Jack had used to kill it and picked the snake up, holding it far away from me as I carefully crossed the road.

Suddenly my devilish, prankish side came out, and, when I stepped into Mrs. Williams' yard I tossed the snake at her. I had never before heard such a startling and horrifying scream. There she stood, swinging her arms and twisting herself up in her freshly-laundered white sheets, until she was almost immobilized. I didn't know where the snake was and the clothesline was on the ground. Mrs. Williams continued to yell angry threatening words about what she would tell my aunt and I should be punished and sent back home. Of course, I ran and didn't stop until I was out of the reach of her voice.

Aunt Nell was always patient and kind to me. I was fascinated by her speech with perfect diction and her attention to her personal details. Whenever she went to town in a pretty, flowered dress she adorned herself with a hat, gloves, and a purse swinging over her wrist. She was very dark with piercing eyes and a wide nose. Her lips were thin, forming a small mouth. She walked with quick short steps, swaying hips, and her head and chin well above the fold of her neck, seemingly in defiance of what her neighbors thought of her. It mattered not to her. She thought of them as mindless and boring. After all, in 1903 she was the first Negro to graduate from Lebanon High School. Her graduation picture hung on her bedroom wall. I was always so curious about all those white girls in the photograph and my very dark-skinned aunt.

Uncle Jack was a short, stocky, brown-skinned-man with bow legs. He had a raspy voice that rumbled from the corner of his mouth around his cigar, and he still managed a smile. He had a twinkle in his eyes. He never had much to say about anyone else's business. He would always say, "It is not for me to judge. Nell, you should stop being so fussy about everything."

I discovered an old newspaper article about the Culver Comics baseball team in 1912, bringing baseball fame to Culver. My uncle Jack, Coleman Jackson, was the catcher and the center of attraction, the article read. There was a picture of him with his team. The article went on to say: "He was stocky, fearless, quick as lightning, and reminded his fans of Roy Campanella, the wonderful Brooklyn Dodgers' catcher. His great sense of humor helped a lot when it came to 'jockeying' the batters."

I loved my Uncle Jack so much and always would follow him and want to know where he was off to. "Come on, Cricket (his nickname for me), let's go down to the pier and work on the boat. We're going fishing in the morning," he would say. That sounded like fun, except I knew I had to get all those slimy worms on my fishing hook. I even had to find my own worms and save them. After catching fish I wanted to save them too, so I would take them home in a bucket of water. I'd then fill the bath tub and watch them swim around before taking them back down to the lake. Then my Aunt Nell made this ghastly discovery and made me stop. I loved my Aunt, too, but in a different way. It was Uncle Jack who taught me to fish and to row a boat. He taught me a lot about the behavior of snakes, and he always defended my appetite for pranks.

Carol age nine.

It was in Lake Maxinkuckee where I learned to swim, even after the water moccasin swam in front of me, sending me splashing and bolting from the water. And this is the lake where I bragged to my friends about my swimming skills: jumped from the pier into deep, unfamiliar water, facing a very challenging swimming feat, returning to my friends with embarrassment and shame.

The Monon Railroad Company tracks ran parallel to Lake Maxinkuckee and all the way to the park where my friends and I attended art, craft and swimming classes every summer. The trains seldom traveled through Culver. Every day the children played skipping and running games all the way down the tracks to the park. It was quality time and growth for a city child. It was learning about my extended family and having a special friend like Thelma Lilly Hodges. It was a chance to understand how wonderful life was even if we did live near the railroad tracks, but feeling we were not any different from the rich children on the other side of the lake. This was the beginning of my strong self-identity that would carry me through life, thanks to Mama, Aunt Nell, Uncle Jack, and 203 Hawkins Street.

A MAGICAL HOLIDAY

One day in December, I walked into my second-grade classroom where I was assigned as a substitute teacher. I looked forward to meeting the children and hoped we could accomplish a lot, enjoy our day, and complete our lesson plan. The classroom was decorated for the Christmas holidays and the children were beyond excited.

Sitting at my desk, I started reading the lesson plan and instructions for that day. A young woman appeared and introduced herself as my assistant. This was good news and a great relief. Having an assistant would give me more quality time with the children. I had 23 energetic and impatient little boys and girls.

The room was noisy and some of the children were not sitting at their desks. As I tried to calm and organize them for our first lesson, I noticed a little girl who was going from desk to desk, tormenting everyone she came near. I had no idea where she was sitting. She hit and pushed children and snatched things from their desks, never saying a word. I noticed her face looked deformed from the swelling around her mouth. I asked my assistant if she could speak and she said, "Yes she can, but she probably won't. Her name is Samantha."

Suddenly, I noticed a little fellow who was autistic and had perched himself on a high window ledge. I was informed by one of the children that he usually stayed there all day. I tried coaxing him down, but my efforts were to no avail. What a challenge this day was going to be! During the reading lesson, the little autistic boy started talking, looking directly at me. I acknowledged him with a smile, calling his name and thanking him for his input.

In my first reading class Samantha would not participate; instead, she was on the floor being dragged by my teaching assistant, who was pulling her by both her legs. Samantha remained silent and very stubborn. I was shocked and dismayed by what I had witnessed. I knew I must make time to reach out to her as soon as possible. Somehow I needed to help make a little girl's holiday better—if only for one day.

Later that day, I noticed Samantha looking at story books. I walked over and stood beside her. Then I asked, "What books do you like to read?" (I first had to give her the control over what I had in mind.) She slowly picked a book from the shelf without ever answering me or looking up. She just held it in her hand for a moment. I said, "Would you like me to read this book to you?" She politely and almost shy-like responded with a nod of her head, as she handed me the book. The amazing fact was that no semblance of a bratty child was evident.

"Come over to the rocking chair, Samantha," I said, and held out my hand; but she didn't reach out. She quietly followed me to the chair and sat down beside me. I didn't quite know what to expect, but I was just delighted and excited we had gotten this far. For sure I knew she was not familiar with love and tenderness.

I first talked about the title and the cover of the book, and described the pictures. I had gotten her attention so far.

As I opened the book, she continued to sit quietly. Then I told the story, the word "magical" came to mind. I started embellishing and adapting the story to her. I was sure the author would understand my reasons and forgive me.

Adding the word "magical" to any series of events in the story convinced her how powerful the magic was. She sat quietly, taking in every word. I told her that sometimes we must believe that things we thought would never come to us will, some day. Believing would make things better—like a better flavor of ice cream.

I knew that something was seriously wrong in her home. She was so full of pain, fear and anger. If things didn't improve soon, she could easily lose her way. She started talking to me about the magic and how much she liked the magic. It was the Christmas holiday season and my heart ached so much for Samantha. As she continued to talk to me, asking questions about the story, I noticed her face didn't look swollen and her mouth was normal. She was so cute. I commented how pretty she was, and she had just made something magical happen. She smiled.

Samantha wanted me to read another book to her, but there just wasn't time. I reminded her that it would soon be Christmas and she already had her first magical gift, and she did this all by herself. For the rest of the day, she was very quiet and nice to all the children and her face remained lovely.

Before I left for the day, Samantha asked, "Miss Carol, will you be back tomorrow?" I looked into her big sad eyes and had to tell her I was sorry I wouldn't and then gave her a hug. I reminded her that we have magical memories which we carry all through our lives, so just keep believing. I think of Samantha and her magical face change every Christmas holiday and wonder—

THE LITTLE HOUSE
IN THE CUL DE SAC

It seemed the fear of homelessness was no longer apparent. The one-story frame-and-brick house was the smallest in the new development. The other homes were all two stories. The building of the house was being closely watched by the intended inhabitant. He carefully followed his father's request, just as he always had done.

The interior of the house was decorated in tan shades with off-white trimming on the wood molding. Off from the breakfast room and kitchen was a large sliding glass door, where the bright morning sun created a perfect place to start the day.

I had become so attached to this little house because I was involved in a lot of the planning from the moment the lot was purchased. This particular style house was perfect for a single person, but large enough for a small family.

I remember all the fun weekends spent looking at furniture for the breakfast room, living room, bedrooms and all-purpose room. I assisted in selecting the flooring, appliances and hardware. Later, a deck was added because of the small sloped backyard.

But before this great little house, in the cul de sac, could be occupied, it became the house that would be the source of troubling and strange behavior, frightening memories and frantic helplessness.

The inside appearance of this home soon took on spiritual energy that was hostile, angry and deadly; it would be the beginning of frightening moments that changed lives forever.

This is a story about mental illness.

For over eight years I struggled to understand a deafening and frightening chaos in my life. Finally relenting, I joined a support group in my city. This was recommended by friends who were familiar with my struggle and pain. I attended with many preconceived ideas and beliefs that they couldn't help me and would only make matters worse. In later years I learned to draw on their strengths and not feel alone and so frightened.

It was a sunny, warm Saturday afternoon on May 22, 2010 when a 43-year-old man crashed his car into two people causing death and serious injury . . . . altering forever the lives of two families.

On a major thoroughfare with several miles of median, a hearing-impaired mother and daughter were standing on the median with signs advertising a car wash being held for their deaf school, when suddenly an SUV, with no warning, plowed into their defenseless bodies. There was no mechanical failure, just a deliberate and deadly aim by the driver.

Almost three months later on August 6, 2010, on this same street, once again a life was taken. On this date one person died and two were seriously injured. These victims were struck down just a few miles from the first deadly accident. Only this time it was an on-duty police officer plowing his car into three motorcyclists. To some, this appeared to be a deliberate act for reasons not yet determined by the court.

I had been away from home for almost two weeks. I was returning with our new baby to Warrington, England (1967) on a World War II C-47 after giving birth to our son in an Air Force hospital two hundred miles from London.

It was a frightening and rough trip returning home because of the electrical storm we had to fly through. I remember the shaking and rattling, and the pouring rain practically drowning out sounds of any voice.

Next to me was my new baby in an infant carrier. The exterior, brightly decorated with toys, animals and balloons, was buckled by the seat belt. The child was sleeping soundly through the storm. Suddenly there was a burst of thunder and then lightening, and I saw flames leaping from the motor on my side as I looked out the window. I screamed and the Air Force flight attendant hurried to my seat. There were just a handful of passengers on the plane. It was used only for service men and their families traveling from Scotland, England and Germany every two weeks to the hospital.

The attendant came over and asked if I was okay, then said she would check with the pilot and tell him about the flames I had seen from the motor. To this day, I can so vividly remember the bright yellow and orange flames and the fear I felt from my heart to my stomach for my new baby.

When the attendant returned from speaking to the pilot, she assured me everything was okay. I just relaxed the best I could in a situation like this. I only wanted to be safely on land and in our home.

When we landed, waiting on the tarmac was my husband, the military doctor who had arranged for my trip, and our family friend from London with her beautiful golden retriever. The doctor, who would be returning to the hospital on the plane, was delighted to greet us and see the new baby. Everyone was just ecstatic and relieved that we had arrived safely.

Years later, I remembered the opening scene in the 1977 television mini-series Roots when Kunta Kinte is born in West Africa; he was cradled in his father's hands and held high up toward the stars.

Long before the Roots miniseries, I witnessed this ancient African tradition of the proud father holding his son high above his head for a few moments, and then in a revered and almost sacred manner, looking up as if offering him to someone greater than himself. I always wondered what he must have been thinking, but I never asked. I couldn't have known what a strong influence he would have over his son's life.

Over twenty years ago my son was diagnosed with paranoid schizophrenia. It was a heartbreaking blow. His father and I were divorced and always had opposite views on how to advise our son. Learning about our son's brain disorder only intensified his dad's determination to have control despite little understanding about anything he deemed a human flaw. Translation: denial.

My son had the human hunger of wanting to be successful and making his parents proud of him. He had been taught about the rewards of being successful, but the disease was unrelenting and advancing. All we could hope for was that it could be controlled with medication and psychotherapy, so he could live a productive and fulfilling life working, being around family and enjoying personal relationships and friendships.

During one of my son's conversations with me he stated, "Mom I'm glad I had a chance to graduate from college."

"Yes, honey, I'm happy you did too," I replied. He was on the Dean's List for most semesters and selected to appear in *Who's Who in America*. "Maybe someday you will be somewhere helping others because of your college education and all the wonderful experiences you had as a child growing up."

I always wanted to give him hope.

Carol and Derek

He then said, "I'm so afraid I could be homeless someday like so many of the mentally ill I see on the streets."

Surprised and shaken by this remark, I said to him, "Don't ever fear being homeless because your family will always make sure this doesn't happen." Hearing him reveal this fear, I experienced a scary possibility that this could happen when his parents were no longer alive.

After his graduation from college he never returned to live in California, so I was the parent living thousands of miles away and was not always aware of what a toll the disease was having on him. As it progressed, he became more and more paranoid.

Coping with day-to-day problems and feelings can sometimes prove to be overwhelming for a mentally ill person. Stress comes in the form of disappointment, rejection and unpleasant surprises, sometimes causing relapse. Now that I look back on the fatal Saturday afternoon, I recognized many of the above symptoms had reared their ugly heads in one form or another for him.

My son was interested and fully involved in every human activity that was good. He was such a loving and pleasant child to bring up. In his adult life, he attended church regularly, sang in the choir and went to bible study every week. He donated monthly to his favorite charity, "Feed the Children." He attended his college reunions as often as he could and always donated to his alumni association. As a young child and teenager he was involved in several sports: track, karate and skiing. He was elected president of his youth branch of *All Seasons Ski Club.*

As a young man he enjoyed social activities and involving himself in the culture of the city. The music he loves spans the gamut from spirituals and R&B to Andrea Bocelli and Il Divo. He had a great appreciation for art and literature that always filled his place of residence. He enjoyed the theatre.

He took pleasure in political discussions and following current-day events. He took his civic responsibilities seriously. I remember when he turned 21 how excited he was about changing his dual citizenship in order to be eligible to vote. It makes me very sad when I think about him not being able to vote.

After college, he was employed in Washington, D.C., for a city councilman and volunteered for President Bill Clinton after passing a tough clearance. He enjoyed the political world and his employment in the Washington government. He also worked for the D.C. school district just before his illness became more evident. His dream to be a good citizen and contribute to his community exists to this day.

During those turbulent years he was admitted to law school and was enrolled at Howard University for graduate work, but the disease was too overpowering for him to succeed.

His dad insisted on his finding something in "middle management" instead of encouraging his son to follow whatever he could handle and be successful at. This caused a lot of pressure and unhappiness for him and certainly heightened all my anxieties.

I talked to my son about starting a business and working from home. He seemed to be amenable to this idea. I knew he could never function in a high-pressure office environment. His pleasant and polite manner often attracted friendships and left people he met feeling that he was loyal, caring, and trustworthy. These were certainly good attributes for self-employment.

Our desires for our son's welfare were definitely our daily concern. As his coping abilities diminished, he moved into a residential treatment facility. For a time, he seemed to be doing better there.

Then, one day, I learned that his father and uncle had decided to move my son from the private treatment facility in another state to be near me and my family. They made the decision that it would be better for him. He had always enjoyed visiting with us. The Christmas before he arrived here to stay, he had spent about two weeks with me. But once again the final decision was not left up to him. He said, "Mom, Dad didn't even ask me if I wanted to move."

I strongly disagreed with any move. My son didn't seem to think he had much of a choice since his dad paid for everything; and this arrangement allowed him to live off his modest disability check. I remember screaming my disagreement, but I knew I couldn't win. I always tried to protect my son from the knowledge that his dad and I were on opposite sides of almost any decision about him.

After he arrived in March 2009, he was happy. Seeing him adjust to his new environment, I felt that Indianapolis was going to be a new beginning for him. At least I hoped it would be a new start for the two of us. I would now have the time to get to know my soon-to-be 42 year-old son much better. Little could I have known then that I would get to know the person my son had become by sitting in an empty house that belonged to him, going through, for more than two months, what seemed to be hundreds of personal papers, books, folders, pictures, awards, plaques and an elegant collection of clothes. Not once did I find any materials that would be morally unacceptable to a mother. I was proud of who and what he had struggled to become.

I had recently experienced a similar situation: spending weeks and weeks sorting through my mother-in-law's personal things after her death in 2008. This was all so surreal and so sad to have the same experience again, but this time it was for a living individual who could no longer take care of his own personal needs.

He had always carried himself in a professional manner. His associates were bright and ambitious thinkers and doers. Since childhood he had surrounded himself with friends who had dreams of college and good jobs. But he also held strong beliefs about helping those who were barely holding on to their fragile dreams or hopes.

Success is an important part of life—we all seek it. I watched his failed dreams turn him into a person empty of important beliefs; stripped of the emotions we should have and share about our lives. He discovered, no matter how hard he tried, that his dreams never seemed to be within his reach.

For many individuals, the illness, or the medication, causes a decline in cognitive abilities. Life becomes a starting over and over again struggle. My son's early work experience and skill sets became obsolete while struggling with the illness. He attended computer schools for years, including vocational rehabilitation courses and job fairs, but the disease robbed him of the professional opportunities which he still dreamed about, and what his father still wanted. He sank deeper and deeper into the abyss of failure until hope often disappeared.

There's a little story I like to tell about 'Hope' . . . .

Man can live about 40 days without food, ten days without water, about three minutes without air, but he cannot live one minute without hope.

In this country, treatment and services for the mentally ill sometimes borders on a national disgrace. Our jails are now filled with the mentally ill. Jails have become the new hospitals. In many ways this country's treatment and understanding of mental illness in our court system and within the general population is not much different than it was in the 19th and 20th centuries. Often times, the mental health care community doesn't adequately follow-up with patients. The provider is not allowed, by law, to talk with the families unless they have a signed release. This flaw in the system renders the provider unable to engage in early detection of relapse for many former patients.

Perhaps in my son's case lives could have been saved if the system had been designed to include interviews with family members. For months I witnessed my son slowly slipping away, and there was no one in mental health services for me to approach about my fears.

Sometimes, social prejudice and family environment can be at the core of a mentally ill person's difficulties. So often the mentally ill are unable to remain free of being drawn into dangerous situations by individuals with dishonest intentions or plans to harm them or others. This happened to my son over ten years ago while he was experiencing a psychotic episode. He was blamed for a crime he did not commit. Too often this country can be harsh and unforgiving, especially when dealing with the mentally ill. The stigma of the disease is tremendous.

I am now helpless to do much to help my son or assist him with his illness, except to tell his story and write the truth so that the whole person is understood. His life was about much more than that fated day on May 22, 2010.

The time I spent going through my son's personal items allowed me the opportunity to glean information that assisted his attorneys in building their defense for mental illness. I am grateful for all their hard work and understanding. My focus and determination keep me balanced and strong enough to do what I can. So I do what I do for my son and for myself, wanting never to forget all the wonderful hours we spent together—having meals, attending special family events and exploring the city. I remember always saying to myself . . . *I wonder if this is going to be the last time we will ever enjoy ourselves like this.* So I cherish those moments.

As of this time, my son has been incarcerated for almost two years awaiting his trial. In the case of the police officer, he only spent about six hours in detention at the county jail and was released. Unlike my son, he is getting whatever help and treatment he needs until his trial.

I don't intend to imply that all jails fail to do their best to service the mentally ill. Sometimes they have an almost impossible job to do. I know that my son receives the best services they have and that the personnel can provide for him in the facility where he is—I am grateful.

My heartfelt thanks to those loving and understanding families and friends who prayed for the victims and sent donations. I hold dear to my heart the young girl who died because of my son's mental illness and the loss and suffering her mother and family are experiencing. So many lives have been shattered forever.

Without the help and friendship of all the wonderful and caring members of NAMI (National Affiliation for Mental Illness), I don't believe I could be where I am and doing what I do today.

What does hope look like? It is inspiration overcoming desperation.

Shortly after the completion of this story, I learned that the judge will soon sign a court order for my son to be admitted to a mental hospital for evaluation and treatment.

THE CALENDAR

After years of being inundated with negative information about Oakland, I developed a mentality of denial. Sometimes when I was outside of Oakland and I was asked by people my place of residence, I would always say, "the East Bay or in the San Francisco area." I discovered my friends were also doing the same thing. This behavior did not make me feel very good about myself because it was wrong. I know wonderful families who raised their children in Oakland including my own son, who is a graduate of Morehouse College. But the emphasis has always been on sensationalizing the bad deeds of our children. I believe that approximately 90% of the youths are doing well. It is the other 10% we hear about that consumes our minds and shapes our beliefs.

I pondered many years over what I could personally do to make the people of Oakland (including myself) feel better about the place where we live. I wanted to try and help improve the image of Oakland—in the flatlands. Oakland had become the "whipping boy" and the "big joke" all across this country. Many of us were struggling with so much anger and despair about the decline of the African-American family.

One day in my home, while looking through the Ebony magazine, I read the section about the African-American youth most likely to succeed, along with their beautiful pictures and profiles. Why couldn't this be done in Oakland, with our youth, to combat the negative images? Why not bring "the good news" to Oakland? I had never published anything in my life, and, I had no idea where to start. Then suddenly it just seemed as if spiritual direction was within my understanding. I knew the format would be a calendar entitled **"Positive Images of Oakland."**

Now, how could I promote my idea? Where could I get the funds for producing such a piece? Where could I find a team of artists to work with me? There were so many questions that should have frightened me, but I had no fear—just passion and determination. My dream soon became a vision and then I started developing a plan. I never understood why there was not a moment of doubt within me. I just knew it could be done.

In October of 1996 my calendar for Oakland rolled off the press after two years of planning, raising over $7,000 and putting together one of the most talented and impressive production teams in the Bay Area. The team consisted of a nationally-renowned photographer from Palo Alto, her graphic design artist from San Francisco, and a printing company from Emeryville. It was truly "our baby" we gave life to after nine months of production work. We celebrated—at the printing company—until wee hours in the morning. It was proof that anything is possible with enough faith and love for what you so deeply believe in. That year, the calendar won its first award—*The San Francisco Silver Award in Recognition of Printing Excellence.*

Carol at printing company examining first calendar run.

This project had revealed for me something I puzzled over for years. Once I was asked by a program trainer what was my purpose in life. Suddenly the word "legacy" had popped into my head. I did not understand what this meant to my life. Was there something else I should do besides being a good mother, citizen and working hard at my job? Was it "the calendar?"

We showcased twelve very beautiful and outstanding youth and young adults in our city for the first time ever. They ranged from high school honor students to an Oakland policeman to a college graduate selected to attend the fourth United Nations World Conference in China. Diana, my niece, Miss January on the calendar and an honor student at Alameda's St. Joseph Notre Dame High School, says, "The calendar shows young people who have risen above the stereotypes most people associate with Oakland."

The calendar designs and colors were stunning. We had a lot to smile and feel good about. This calendar for the non-profit group was a beautiful work of art with extraordinary black-and-white photography. It also contained important information about the dreams and good works of each calendar subject. There were lots of others who also found "the calendar idea" quite attractive and good news in print. Eller Media Company donated BART poster space all the way to San Leandro, the Oakland Tribune ran a front-page story, and Channel 5 TV station did a segment on their evening news.

I had the support of such well-known leaders as the current-Governor Jerry Brown of California and U.S. Congresswoman Barbara Lee.

The calendar was a new idea that brought a breath of fresh air for many people. The young people were so proud and grateful to be recognized by the elders of their community. They were nominated by their teachers, counselors, friends and parents for academics, leadership skills, community service and extra curricular activities. And my life had been changed forever. For the next six years these young people were the pride of Oakland and the center of my life. They live on in the History Room of the main Oakland Library, along with other calendar subjects, featured in subsequent years in the *Positive Images of Oakland Calendar*.

There was nothing more wonderful than showcasing the accomplishments of our youth of Oakland by acknowledging them in a format that had never been attempted before. Reality doesn't necessarily make me a disbeliever, so I am always somewhere between being an idealist and a realist. I once read where Martin Luther King described tough-minded individuals as persons who could balance realism and idealism.

They, like me, have tough minds and at the same time soft hearts. These young people were given a voice and a venue to proclaim their greatness.

Carol L. Evans and Johnnie Cochran Jr.,
at the Gingerbread House Sunday brunch in his honor.

THE OAKLAND TRIBUNE
1996 - 2002

Oakland church calendar honors high achievers

"When I came to Oakland from Indianapolis in 1971," Evans-Conley said, "I noticed how reluctant some of us were to say that we were from Oakland. We would say the Bay Area, the East Bay or the San Francisco Bay Area. I wanted to make a contribution that would help us be proud of our city."

Youth the focus

OAKLAND — All in all, Carol Evans Conley's ordeal with recognizing young, positive role models has been rewarding.

"There is nothing in Oakland that is published with 12 pages of something positive that represents the grass-roots people in Oakland, who work hard, pay taxes, struggle to get their kids to college," said Carol Evans Conley, development associate for the 20-year-old grass-roots organization. "There is nothing that really represents that. The calendar is our way of showcasing our young people, bringing good news to the community."

Calendar showcases city's positive images

By Victoria Hudson
STAFF WRITER

OAKLAND — Instead of a man for all seasons, an Oakland nonprofit group has discovered an entire population, reflected in its 1997 "Positive Images of Oakland" calendar which goes on sale today.

Said to be a first for the city and the nonprofit Oakland Community Organizations, the calendars are expected to raise $50,000, which will be spread among various community groups. The OCO is a federation of 32 congregations and neighborhood groups.

The 1997 calendar features 12 local young adults, ages 16 to 30, nominated by their community for academic, personal and professional accomplishments. The youths represent some of the best Oakland has to offer, said Carol Evans Conley, OCO project director. Media portrayals often distort the more common and positive contributions of Oakland's young people, preferring in-stead to focus on crime and other nega tive aspects, Evans Conley said.

"We want to bring good news to th community," she said. "We've got thou sands doing so many good things. Thi

Please see **Calendar**, A-1

Free 2003 calendar to celebrate Oakland's 150 years of history

Conley said she hopes to take people on a scenic tour of Oakland's past and present, to "use your positive imagination for the future."

Each month is a collage of five images or more. In January, travelers will journey to places that expand their knowledge of the world, such as the Oakland Museum of California, Oakland

MEMORIES OF JANET

The time I spent with Janet will always be etched in my heart and mind because I considered it such quality time. It was a life experience that prepared me for greater challenges. I did so enjoy using my imagination and creativity to gently encourage Janet to become more independent, and to try and enjoy the life she was given. Her journey was not always comfortable, predictable or easy because she had fewer tools to use than most of us.

Janet was a mildly retarded, manic-depressive, 55-year-old woman. She was of average height and slightly overweight with short, reddish-brown hair. She never wore make-up or jewelry. Janet wore wire-framed glasses and was a smoker. She loved to walk and she often walked for blocks and blocks, so she had to wear very sturdy, comfortable walking shoes in order to help balance her wobbly gait.

Janet lived at a private residential facility for mentally challenged adults, both women and men, located in Oakland, California. Their living arrangements consisted of homes with 24-hour staff and independent living apartments with only daytime staff. Janet lived in the apartments with another client. Throughout her life she had lived in several different facilities. Her therapist believed she had been sexually molested in one of the earlier places where she had lived.

Deep inside herself Janet was very unhappy with how she looked. I once asked her to draw pictures of how she thought she looked and how she would prefer to be. That's when I discovered the sadness she had with her appearance. She felt this part of her life was controlled by her family, like what she wore and having her hair cut.

There are many Janet stories, some happy and fun, some sad and painful, just like many of our own stories. Janet was usually pretty clear about what she wanted for herself and what she did not want in her life. It was just always so painful for me to watch her not having many options for herself. But, at the same time, I was grateful to be the one who helped her with her independence.

Whenever Janet would find something to laugh about, it was just a joy to hear her chuckle. I can so clearly remember joyful, child-like sounds she sometimes made at the end of her brief sentences. She would speak to you with only a few words, so you had to listen intently to try and understand the full meaning and expression of whatever it was she was trying to convey. I spent a lot of time doing that and then I would usually repeat what I thought I understood, and believe me she knew how to express "No" if you didn't get the drift of her thoughts.

Janet had much difficulty with reading, comprehension, problem-solving, her attention span and sometimes her memory. During her manic stages she would wander off to bars and indulge in inappropriate social behavior with men, and wasteful spending of her money. During these times she was put at the mercy of those who cared little for her. I'm sure she was longing for attention and love.

She would sometimes mention the difference between her two parents. Her mother seemed to never accept her many limitations and would quickly lose patience with her—quite often, blurting out cruel criticisms. But then her father would show understanding and compassion for Janet and always use endearing terms to comfort and please her.

Janet quickly discerned the difference between her mother's and father's place in her life. Her mother's inability to accept her caused many painful emotions, so much so, that her worst demons were the memories she had of her mother. On each anniversary of her mother's death she would often need to be hospitalized. This was the "coming down" side of her mental illness. She was haunted by the fact that her mother had died before she was able to tell her mother how much she loved her, and that she had forgiven her.

My contract with Janet's family included a monthly expense account to be used for travel, entertainment, restaurants and any other leisure activity I considered important. My job requirement was to coach Janet into having better personal hygiene, healthier eating habits, and to help her with a housekeeping routine. She had resisted the efforts of the staff at her facility to help her.

Our weekend activities would always be something that could stimulate all her senses in a way that would relax her and make her smile. I always liked it when Janet would smile because with that smile would be her chuckle. Along with these moments, I would always make sure she could just vent, if that was what she needed to do. When someone would just listen to her it would be a comforting moment in her life. That's when you might get a longer-than-usual Janet communication experience.

The story I like best took place in the therapist's office where I first met Janet. I had been scheduled for an interview with her therapist of eight years, and I remember saying how important I thought it would be for Janet to also interview me. Because if for some reason she didn't like me, then there would be nothing we could accomplish.

Her therapist had helped prepare her for this interview, and had given her a list of questions. She had warned me that Janet would be very shy and nervous. It was a great moment in my life that reminded me of my humility and this incredible honor.

Before Janet started her questions, what I remember the most was how she hung her head and slowly peered over her eyeglasses at me, with her composed fear. I must have put on the biggest smile I have ever made in my life. The positive energy flowed! I was hoping she would actually be able to feel it as I did. I knew right then that this was an opportunity in our lives that we just had to make work, for the both of us.

The questions were difficult for Janet, but she managed quite well and I attempted to give Janet a great introduction to me. After that interview, I remember lots of smiles and feelings about "let's just get started."

Our activities included movies, dining out, museums, walks and volunteering at the SPCA, caring for the little kittens and walking the dogs. Long before I had ever heard anything about the calming effect animals had on the elderly, helping them with their depression, I just thought Janet would be happy around animals she could care for.

I think it gave her the feeling of being needed. I often had to help with the not-so-fun kind of things, like their computer projects. The board members invited us to their annual fundraiser, held outside in the gardens. Janet and I assisted with the food, beverages and greeting the guests. It was a wonderful experience for both of us.

There is one more story I would like to share. It is the one about our weekend getaway. I came up with the bright idea of pretending we would have a make-believe weekend trip. I made reservations at one of our hotels on the waterfront in Jack London Square. We were both excited about packing a few things and getting away from our usual weekend view of people and places.

Well! It just wasn't comfortable for Janet. All of a sudden she was spending the night in a strange place and bed. She never slept all night. She paced the floor and would go out on the balcony and mumble about the moon. It was frightening her. She was experiencing strange and unsettling feelings. Dear God, if I only knew what she was thinking and feeling. Needless to say, we returned home that next morning in a state of distress—I, because of my guilt and disappointment with myself for spoiling Janet's weekend, and Janet because of being confused and unhappy about everything. I was afraid she would never trust me again, but our lives together continued as if nothing had occurred to interrupt our spiritual rhythms.

I was most grateful for the few times I was able to get inside Janet's mind. She shared things with me about her feelings, and what had hurt her most, like the fears and disappointments she had faced in life. I could only keep assuring her that she could find peace in her life, and we all are capable of forgiving ourselves as well as others forgiving us. I now will end my "Janet Memories" on paper, but never in my heart. She passed in 2002 near Santa Barbara, California.

An essay about Hurricane Katrina victims cast as slaves is masterful as "Katrina: The Ghosts of 1865." *Peggy Stinnett, former writer of the Oakland Tribune.*

Katrina: The Ghosts of 1865 came from my pain, anger, disbelief, and sadness. Writing this essay helped to relieve much of the trauma of what I witnessed from news reports and published articles. Authors say that writing helps you make sense of all the chaos in your life and around you. This is my humble tribute to the fallen and to the heroes and sheroes of hurricane Katrina. They all deserve to remain in our memories and in the oral history we pass on to other generations.

1st Place Winner in 2006 Write On! Senior Creative Writing Contest.

KATRINA:
THE GHOSTS OF 1865

They came, with their only possessions in bags, carts and any container that could be carried or floated. Their haggard bodies and pain-filled faces were haunting to my soul. They walked and walked in the heat of the sun and through stagnant and foul-smelling waters seeking shelter, food and clean drinking water. No plans or provisions had been made for them by the very people who were elected to protect them. Families and individuals were stranded throughout and amongst the ruins of a city. Many were on roof tops or trapped in their homes, or drowned and their bodies were trapped where they last cried out for help. Others were killed and swept away by the flood and left hanging from trees, or floating in the rising waters, or flung on top of some mass wreckage.

I watched in horror this frightening scene that was taking me back to 1865—the end of slavery. My ancestors, after centuries, were finally free from their daily personal pain or cruel and inhumane treatment. Historians tell us that when the Civil War ended, the Southern black people left their plantations by the thousands. Great bedlam appeared with a deadly and desperate slow march, away from their present hell. They would walk for hundreds of miles along dangerous and uncertain paths. They would discard their old, tattered, and filthy slave clothes the first chance they would have. Along the roads would lie the bodies of many who had met their unfortunate demise. There was always danger of a deadly assault. This new idea of freedom for the former slaves (also known as refugees) was very frightening for most of the South.

Could this not be the return of a time in history that I am witnessing? The ghosts of my ancestors loom over this country. These victims of the Katrina flood waters, who were often referred to by the press as "refugees", were just beginning to start living their worst nightmare. They would soon scatter all over the countryside looking for their loved ones, being turned away and around by angry voices spewing ugly words and loud threats. "You can't stay here." "Go back!" "What do you people want?" "There's nothing for you here, go back!" "There is no room here!" "Bang, bang!" "Turn around and go back." These Southern blacks would witness the death of many around them who could no longer wait for unfulfilled promises. It was now up to the living to carry on the painful struggle of reuniting families, finding work, and owning land.

No place to live, rest or be cool—the ghosts of 1865. They must keep traveling to try and reach a safe place, a place where they could have a home. Their lives have been changed forever by the devastation of Katrina and the cruel excuses and deliberate abandonment by heartless individuals. Each day I watched report after report with teary eyes, labored breathing and deep sighing. America's dirty little secret had been exposed, at last, for the whole world to see. All the past generations of deprivation, oppression, prejudice, and racism were unveiling their horrid images right in front of our faces. It seemed as though help would never come to stem this tide of human pain. The Katrina victims started to lose their hope, and my hope hung by a very thin thread. Over and over again I asked myself, how could this happen to any human beings in America in 2005?

It was often difficult for me to get through my day without thoughts and words to try and understand how this would all end, after nature's cruelest assault did not spare the poorest and weakest. Where was their escape? How long would they be trapped in this modern-day forced passage to nowhere for food, water and shelter? I was angry and sad. They were hungry and thirsty! Who was I angry at? How many of the powers-to-be had to know what could happen if the levees ever broke and the lower bottoms were flooded? Because they were mostly poor and elderly, or young and fatherless, or uneducated and unemployed, shouldn't we stop judging them and instead mourn their condition and journey, and pray that they can find some semblance of what had been taken away. But there were those who said, "So be it! All the undesirables and unwanted have been washed out of our city."

Who are they? Where are they? They are our brothers and sisters and children of this human race. They are scattered all over this land with their families and meager belongings in parts and pieces. Here are the ghosts of 1865. They are scattered all over this land—poor, sad and angry. Folks, there is a Katrina waiting for us, all over this land!

DISCOVERING LIFE IN CUBA

My introduction to Cuba was to have been in 1989 when I was employed at a college in Northern California. One of my college professors, a friend, had approached me about traveling with her and a group of students on a trip to Cuba. I was always ready for a great adventure, a learning experience, and an opportunity to meet other people of the world. I believed that I was not only a resident in my city but a citizen of the world. However, it wasn't long before our plans suddenly came to a halt because of what was occurring with a foreign government on the other side of our world—the collapse of the Soviet Union.

What could this have all meant to our planned visit to Cuba? The Cuban economy heavily depended on assistance from Russia because of the U.S. embargo that has been in existence since 1963. To put it simply, this change in the Russian government would probably mean a severe shortage of food supplies and many other essential resources for the Cuban people. The decision was reached that our needs might not be looked after in a situation like that, so our trip would have to be cancelled. Translation: It could be unsafe for us to travel in Cuba.

Modern Cuba is possibly one of the least understood, and most wrongly portrayed, countries in this hemisphere, shrouded in past and present U.S. propaganda. Add to this the forgotten or unknown history of pillage and plunder by pirates; then wars by the Spanish, French and English for the control and occupation of Cuba that brought colonization and corrupt governments. Sadly enough, it is now only remembered for its revolution, and Fidel Castro. The Cuban government is despised and denigrated by the United States government. (Source: *Cuba Ediciones Niocia S.L.*)

More recently, the speeches, celebrations and all the propaganda regarding the possible end coming to the Fidel Castro reign was celebrated by the Cuban-Americans in Florida. Even our U.S. officials in Washington, were seen on television touting examples of how our country would stand by the Cuban people and assist them in having a democratic government, and spreading the usual propaganda about the people and the conditions in Cuba.

Christopher Columbus discovered Cuba on October 28, 1492 and then established Spanish colonies. After slaves were brought to Cuba, cultures, traditions, and foods were merged. In this unforgettable country of 11 million people there are four different ethnic groups: 51% mulatto, 37% white, 11% black, 1% Chinese. Cuba is a multi-racial society with a population of mainly Spanish and African origins. There is a Spanish literacy rate of 95% among the Cuban population.

Among the population are some of the most beautifully-hued and hospitable people. Their exciting music and dance flood the soul and mind with romantic rhythms. Cuba is made up of keys and islets surrounded by the northern Atlantic and Caribbean coastal waters, with beaches of white sand and tropical terrain.

In 1961 Fidel Castro declared Cuba to be a Socialist state. Prior to the revolution, Castro was a member of the democratic parliament, but saw no way to improve the lives of his people under an oppressive government.

After the success of the revolution, his plan for the Cuban people was to make sure everyone would receive an education, have health care, be employed, and have a house to live in. Also, everyone could enjoy the beaches. Before the revolution, most were not educated and the dark-hued Cubans were not allowed on the beaches. Cuba was nothing more than a brothel for the American service men and a haven for gangsters and gambling under Fulgencio Batista.

Cuba's economy consists of some natural resources like nickel, iron ore, copper, salt and timber. Their agriculture is sugar, citrus and tropical fruits, tobacco, coffee, rice, beans, meat, and vegetables. Much of their agricultural production is poor. Rum and the Cuban cigar industry do fairly well, according to recent reports. Oil in Cuba is a new exploratory industry that could work out well for them if they have technical or other production capabilities. Tourism is now the biggest contributor to the Cuban economy.

Cuba's largest organized religion is the Roman Catholic Church. A blend of native African religions and Roman Catholicism is widely practiced in Cuba, which is no longer characterized as an atheist state; people are free to worship however they wish.

Years after the failure of my first opportunity to visit Cuba, a second opportunity presented itself in 2003. One day in the AAA (American Automobile Association) office, I discovered a group was traveling to Cuba with General Tours/Cross-Cultural Solutions in New Hampshire. This organization had approximately 60 days left on an educational license, and then it would not be renewed by the U. S. Treasury Department Office of Foreign Controlled Assets.

At that time, there were five different licenses issued by the U.S. Treasury Department to travel to Cuba: general, educational, humanitarian, professional, and religious.

When this second opportunity presented itself to me, I started planning for the great adventure. Never did I dream of having the chance to travel to Cuba after my first plan was ended so abruptly by the collapse of the Soviet Union. I was drawn to Cuba because I knew it as a place where battles were fought and won, just 90 miles from our borders. These conflicts were fought and won, with the help of Black people, after centuries of oppression and slavery.

ON MY WAY

After all the official procedures were completed, we were on our way to the Republic of Cuba. There were more than 130 in our group, from all over the United States. We would meet in Miami for our 8:30 a.m. flight to Havana. When my trip from California had to be suddenly changed to fly directly to Indianapolis, instead of Miami, because of the death of my uncle. I arrived in Miami from Indianapolis the day before leaving for Cuba, and spent the night near the International Airport.

It was not one of those nights that I slept soundly. We were told to arrive at the airport four hours before our flight. I wasn't sleeping when I heard my alarm clock and the call from the front desk. It would only take me a short while to get ready for my taxicab trip to the airport, where I would board the Marazul Charter Airline flight to Havana. *Did I have everything?* How many times had I asked myself that question? I seemed to be carrying a year's accumulation of papers and documents.

When I arrived, it took a short while to find my gate. There seemed to be no one waiting that I could identify as part of my group. Due to my nervousness, I had arrived before my group was told to check in.

Before long, I noticed people beginning to gather in my vicinity. My eyes quickly darted around, searching for any semblance of conversation or other clues to link me with them. Suddenly I could hear conversations about documents, overweight luggage, the flight, and what to expect when we arrived in Havana. I began to mingle and converse with the crowd as it grew. People appeared friendly, excited and eager to get started on this venture to a part of the world unfamiliar to most Americans. This was a place that my country did not want me to be.

Now where was our group leader?

Suddenly appearing among us was a gentleman carrying an armload of papers and a briefcase. This had to be the representative from General Tours—perky, buoyant and with a big smile. As he began to make announcements my brain started racing almost at a runaway pace, thinking of my arrival in Cuba and what the next eight days would be like. Everything went smoothly and we boarded the plane. I then found my seat, after placing my carry-on above. This flight of approximately 45 minutes would take me to a place I had only dreamed about. Upon arrival I would find people of my skin color and hear music I would recognize and love. I would discover new foods and the Cuban culture—past and present—to sample and savor.

The short flight was smooth and enjoyable. We had very good weather. When we left Miami the temperature was in the high 70's, clear and virtually no wind. As far as I was concerned the day could not have been better.

At 9:30 a.m. we arrived at the José Marti Airport, named after the man known as the "Father of the Revolution." The airport was a huge one-story metal structure with lines and lines of people arriving from all over the world. I was listening to the many languages and feeling the excitement about where I was. Even though I couldn't understand the languages, I wasn't feeling as though I was a stranger in a strange land. I felt that all our hearts spoke the language of love for this country.

Day One

We were met at the airport by our program representative after clearing customs. As I stood in line, I focused on the faces of beautifully-hued people and strained my ears to hear the language. I wondered who might be Cuban citizens and who might be in my category—inquisitive visitors. I could hardly wait to exit the airport and feel the Cuban experience—to hear the voices and to see the faces of the people, anticipating the adventure of my life, during our time in Cuba.

It was chaos after exiting the airport; people searching for luggage, while discovering blocks and blocks of mini-vans waiting for passengers. I wondered if Cuban travel arrangements would be as organized as my travels in other countries as I tried to figure out which bus I would board. Then I heard the voice of our representative. He was once again frantically waving his arms, with lots of papers flapping around in the air, and motioning for everyone from our group to move toward him. I was traveling alone but, as I explained to my family, there was no trepidation on my part for my safety. Alone only meant I would have a room all to myself.

An hour passed by the time we received information and instructions for our first few days in Havana. We then received our bus assignments and were given several pieces of paper, along with an apology, for changes in our itinerary due to the larger than anticipated group from the United States. This caused me some consternation and difficulty, trying to keep up with all the changes, some occurring day by day.

I didn't pay that much attention to these announcements because I was too busy gathering my luggage and checking to see if I had all my small items, like the tape recorder my brother had showed me how to operate at the airport in Indianapolis. I hoped to be allowed to use it at all our meetings with the Cuban emissaries.

After the bus assignments and instructions were clear, and printed information disseminated, we were on our way to the Presidente Hotel in Havana. It was announced that we would be given a brief city tour, then lunch before arriving at our hotel. I sat next to a window, observing every building and sign; closely watching the people walking on the tree-lined streets. *Where were they going? Were they happy? Where were they employed? What types of houses did they live in with their families?*

Presidente Hotel where we stayed in Havana.

Hammel's Alley is where local Afro-Cuban musicians perform.

Before our arrival at the hotel, we were given our schedules for the rest of our tour. Two schedule changes made many unhappy. The visit to the School of Social Work was cancelled as was one to Hammel's Alley, where we were to meet with African-Cuban musicians. We later learned the changes had to do with the unexpectedly large size of our group.

There seemed to be countless announcements, but I just couldn't focus on much of anything that was taking place on our bus. I did hear the message about meals scheduled in private homes nestled in the lush green hills. I was so anxious to plant my feet on the ground and have my first close look at Cuba—to savor the foods and move to music I had long dreamed about. But first, there was an orientation at 6:00 p.m. in the hotel dining room to meet our representative from *Cross Cultural Solutions,* and our first formal introductions to members of our group. As we looked each other over and conversed, I pondered over the reasons we were all there concluding our reasons would be similar, even with our different backgrounds and origins and unique personalities.

That evening, we traveled to a seafood restaurant, Don Cangrejo in Havana. During dinner I met Evora Jordan, who happened to join my group at our dinner table. She is a writer and community activist, and we agreed to stay in touch. The writing she does reminded me of Angela Lansbury, the star of one of my favorite Sunday television programs, "Murder She Wrote." She even came from Maine, the same area in which this story was filmed. We all expressed our delight with our first seafood Cuban dinner. That night we returned to our hotel and were in agreement that this seafood experience was a great starter.

Seafood shipments from the United States ceased in 1959 and just started again the year we arrived. For many years after the revolution, food was very difficult to import from other countries. I remember wondering why we never had chicken breasts with our meals, only legs and thighs. We assumed the better parts of the chicken were saved and served to the elite. However; since returning from Cuba, I understand that the embargo, along with the fall of the Soviet Union, interrupted Cuba's food supply.

Day Two

The morning after my first night's sleep in Cuba I arose, looked out my window and watched the school children lining up on the walkway across from my hotel. They were patiently waiting for the school doors to open. It was early morning, and it was very pleasant to be awakened by the joyful chatter. After a few moments my eyes took in the panoramic view of the Havana skyline. Not too bad after stories I had heard of buildings crumbling because of the neglect by the Communist government and abject poverty in Cuba.

View from hotel window of the Havana skyline.

Our first breakfast was hardy and delicious: fruits, breads, juice, breakfast meats, rice and most of the condiments I normally have. The large sunny room had huge windows that looked out onto the Olympic-size pool, with many lounge chairs and tables with umbrellas. After breakfast we would leave for the Harbor of Havana. My friend Evora looked rested and perky.

We exchanged smiles and chatted briefly about how comfortable our rooms were. Evora was an unpretentious, short, plump woman of about 70 years. She wore wire-framed glasses and talked with a New England dialect.

"Carol, would you like to go on a search with me to find a DVD of the history of Cuba?" she asked. "I have been told I can get it from the Cuban Office on Culture."

"Sure, of course, I'd love to go with you. When do you plan on going?" I said while finishing my breakfast.

"The first time we have a few free hours," Evora said, while she finished eating her sweet roll. "I want to write about my adventure in Cuba."

I thought to myself that this would give us a chance to explore on our own. What fun we could have, submerging ourselves in the culture of Cuba.

That morning our first stop was at the "Square of the Revolution" where, we learned, the revolution had begun. There stood a huge monument, a statue with a modernistic style, dedicated to the national hero José Marti. We learned this was the tallest structure in the city. While walking the grounds of "The Square" I couldn't help but have this strange feeling, I would have been part of the revolution if I had been a Cuban. Then we were off to the "Harbor of Havana." My excitement started to build. Old Havana and the Modern Havana are grand tourist attractions. Ancient Havana is the suspended past of old fortresses, sacrosanct temples and cobblestone streets.

Harbor of Havana is a busy place.

Suddenly we were amongst many colorful old American cars which reminded me of a moving antique car show. We were told those cars are kept in impeccably good condition, painted bright colors, and given mirror-shines. A few steps away and we were in Modern Havana with its long promenades and beautiful colonial restored buildings from the 20th century that are hotels and restaurants. That section is also home to government buildings. As we walked, coming down one of the promenades, I stopped to watch a wedding party and took pictures. We also witnessed young people doing all the normal things we enjoy in the United States; lovers at the beach, children happily playing in the parks, elders sitting on park benches, and even a short parade in a celebratory march.

Many of Havana's buildings are striking and charming mansions of colonial architecture. Built in the 1800's, they have been renovated for the pleasure of tourists and the wealthy; a mixture of the past with the modern-day comfort of the present. Many have beautiful gardens and are popular for meetings and romantic rendezvous at night. Many of the restaurants and government buildings we visited had been the private homes of sugar barons. Other buildings were designed and built by the French and Spanish during the latter part of the 19th century and early 20th century.

Mansion once belonged to the United States.

We had lunch in modern Havana at La Dominica, and after lunch we visited the Revolution Museum. This was indeed a most educational and riveting experience, taking us back into the long, ugly history of the Cuban people's struggles for freedom. I carefully and slowly walked through every crowded room of the museum and made my way up to each large exhibit window, stopping to read all the documents. There was just so much to read and remember. One thing I would never forget was the bullet holes still in the wall of the museum from the revolution where some students had fought and died. This was the first time in my life I had ever seen a bullet hole. As we walked down the stairs and past the bullet holes, each step I took I felt there was someone there I needed to step around or over. I could almost envision the young bodies of the students lying on the steps.

Roberto, our travel host and guide, was anxious to take us to where the group would hear about Cuba's vast restoration project. When we arrived, we were shown the architectural model for the restoration campaign. For this reason, the Cuban government stopped the demolition of many of the buildings. The presentation by one of the officials focused on who raises the money for the restoration and how this benefits other parts of the city. It was so exciting having a peek into Cuba's future, and I hoped that this would all come to fruition for them.

Upon returning to our hotel, Joe Villa and his nephew Marcus from California were waiting for me to return. I was happy to see them and enjoyed hearing about their Cuban experience—the sights, sounds and foods we couldn't get enough of. These two had been coming to Cuba for many years. They were on their way to Santiago de Cuba, known as Cuba's most exotic city, rich in the history of the African and Spanish cultures. Unfortunately, my tour did not include this area, but wouldn't that be a reason to return?

DAY THREE

Another great breakfast, and then off to tour the Rum Factory. Once there, we heard a presentation on the production of rum. The building was opened in 1895 and rum became Cuba's most profitable export. We tasted sweet and dry rums. We then had an animated and humorous presentation, about the sales side of the rum business. I think that was to get us all in the mood to shop. Fidel Castro's favorite rums were pointed out and, of course, they were beyond the average person's ability to afford—just nice to look at and wonder about the taste. We were shown another scale model of the new city and listened to a talk on Havana's urban development.

Next we met with a United States desk officer at ICAP (The Cuban Institute of Friendship With The Peoples). This was informative, educational and thought-provoking. Questions were asked by many of the people in the room. This meeting was held in one of the beautifully restored 19th century buildings that once belonged to the United States. There was a speech given by a lady on Cuba's educational system. When she finished, we were invited to ask questions. When I asked if they had a truancy problem, she did not understand the meaning of the word. When I explained, she seemed confused and stunned saying "No. Why would a child not want to attend school?" There was no response from our group. Our comments would have surely been complicated, troubling, and sad.

After lunch, our tour guide stopped for us to visit a cemetery built in 1869. The temperature was mild and it was raining. Everyone just seemed to go with it and listened intently to our guide. The tombs were all above ground like the ones in New Orleans.

Before returning to the hotel we were taken to "Hammel's Alley," a community project that provides and promotes Cuban music and culture. We met with local African-Cuban musicians and artists. The buildings in this area are all painted bright colors with Cuban-African artwork. We met many of the artists, admired the art, and did some shopping while listening to the soul-stirring music and watching the seductive dances.

On the way back to our hotel, we all chatted about the day's experience. I had made another friend and we always sat next to each other and shared stories about our lives. She was a widow. Her husband had been a doctor who, while visiting Argentina, was rushed to the side of a man stretched out on the ground unable to breath. He assisted the man and saved his life. Later, he found out it was the great Cuban icon and revolutionist Che Guevara. While visiting Cuba I had seen pictures and tributes to him, and was anxious to learn more about him. In *The Death of A Revolutionary*, I learned he suffered severely with asthma all his adult life.

That evening, we had dinner at Los Doce Apostoles, a beautiful mansion now a restaurant along the Boulevard. After dinner we were transported to one of the CDRs (Committee for the Defense of the Revolution). Cuban families organized in every neighborhood. The children welcomed us with a performance. Then we were invited inside for refreshments, music, and dance. Everyone was friendly and warm.

I don't know if I was the only one a little disappointed not being able to ask questions of the group about what is the focus of the CDR committees. We had been told this was going to be an opportunity to talk with them. I was later told that a CDR leader was not available to speak with me. Earlier, I learned they closely watch members of their neighborhoods who are not performing their duties—like keeping the streets and parks clean. They were to watch and report anyone having alcohol or drug problems and family difficulties. Everyone must have a job to do. I agreed. We all enjoyed ourselves.

Day Four

This morning we left for our trip to Pinar Del Rio Province. There was a disturbance in front of our hotel that caused me to rise from my seat on our motor coach and look out the window at all the commotion. The Cuban police were speaking angrily to a young man carrying a handful of compact disc. He was trying to deliver them to a lady who had ordered them for a few of us at the jazz club she attended the night before. He was bringing me a CD of the famous Buena Vista Social Club.

Suddenly the lady I had made friends with jumped off our motor coach, rushed to the young man's side, and started explaining to the police the reason he was approaching our hotel was only to deliver the CDs she had paid for. We were told that the Cuban locals are not allowed to come into the hotels unless they are there to work, because they will be arrested. It was quite an experience to witness the heavy hand of the government.

This reminded me of the day Evora and I walked past a large concrete building with few windows and American flags flying. It is called the American Interest Building. When we started to cross to the other side, walking towards the building, we were immediately stopped by the Cuban police motioning for us to go back. I later learned there is a building in Washington, DC named the Cuban Interest Building. I think this was a rather stealthy way to not call them embassies.

The ride to Pinar Del Rio was about one and a half hours long. Most of the time we were the only ones on the highway. This was certainly a new experience for me—nothing like the roads in America. Our guide identified the different types of trees and tobacco fields in this region. We visited a tobacco factory and saw how the tobacco is processed and cigars made by lovely Cuban ladies dressed all in white. Observing them at work seemed as though I was witnessing a sacred ritual and a life-long tradition, handed down from their families and the tobacco barons. The sweet aroma from the tobacco permeated the entire building.

Roberto said we would pick up our specialist guide shortly, but Roberto would remain with us. This was a beautiful area with hills and thick vegetation. It is used as a retreat as well as a residential area. This mountain community is also an artists' colony. We were taken to meet the artists and observe them at work in their studios. As I was making my way through the studios I could hardly contain my excitement—gazing around and taking in as much as possible—when I came upon a young man showing his paintings. I walked up to him and started a conversation about his work when suddenly he asked, "Where are you from?"

"California," I said.

"Where in California?" he asked with excitement in his voice and a broad smile.

"Oakland," I responded.

"I lived in Oakland for two years," he said, "and I attended the College of Arts and Crafts."

"Bowled-over" is the expression I would use to describe my feelings. I was so excited when the young artist started asking about his favorite restaurants and other venues he enjoyed. This was surreal—what we were experiencing together, here in Cuba.

We traveled to one of Cuba's schools in the mountain community and visited with children in grades six and eight. We had a chance to talk with the children about their education, and dreams they had for the future. Some of us had brought school supplies from America, and now we had a chance to give them out. The children were grateful and thanked us (some speaking English). I thought about how the needs of children are the same all over the world. They all need adults to be the keepers of their dreams.

After leaving the school, we traveled to the site of healing sulfur waters, flowing from the blue marble bed of the San Diego River. I was encouraged to put my feet in the waters. After enjoying the clean, cool sulfur waters, we traveled to a charming family restaurant high in the mountains to have our lunch before returning to the hotel.

The healing sulfur waters in the Pinar Del Rio Valley.

DAY FIVE

The next morning, we boarded our motor coach for the agricultural countryside, on our way to the city of Trinidad. We stopped at the famed Villa Clara to tour a monument to Ernesto "Che" Guevara and his comrades. Che was known as a handsome, modern-day romantic figure of the Cuban Revolution.

I was mesmerized by what I found when I entered the mausoleum. The likenesses of their faces were carved on the front of their bronze crypts. Stories of Che's military feats and his approaching demise were displayed in his own handwriting behind large display windows. Che and his men all died in remote areas, far from their home countries. The scene in the mausoleum was solemn, quiet and sometimes rather eerie.

As I stood there I contemplated why I was so enchanted and drawn to Che Guevara and his heroic life and tragic end. When I turned to leave, I couldn't see any of the people on our tour. Then I realized they were all on the bus waiting for me to return. I discovered we had not been told to go into the mausoleum, but just to walk around the square and return to the bus. I felt special because I was the only one from our tour who had the opportunity, or took the opportunity, to have a close-up view of this revered Cuban hero's resting place.

We then traveled to "The Monument of the Derailed Train" in the City of Santa Clara. Leading up to the end of the revolution, the train was carrying ammunition and Batista's army. It was successfully attacked by the leaders of the revolution. The battle ended the revolution. Batista and his immediate family fled to Dominican Republic on January 1, 1959.

Before arriving in Trinidad, we visited the home of a family in the countryside and talked with the lady of the house and the children she was caring for. We were invited to look around. I walked to the kitchen and then out near the back of the house, suddenly a large white pig appeared and started toward me. I screamed and quickly returned to find the others touring the home. That was the biggest pig I had ever seen. I had never seen a white one.

We arrived at our hotel in Trinidad that evening. It was a large, sprawling modern structure built only 15 years before, and stretching across a white sandy beach and the blue, crystal-clear Caribbean Sea.

Trinidad is a city where one walks on cobblestone streets among colonial-style buildings. It is a charming city in the center of the island of Cuba, in the Sancti Spiritus province. It basically remains as it was centuries ago.

School children in the city of Trinidad.

DAY SIX

A small group of us met with two social workers from Havana. This meeting was planned to replace the change in our itinerary. The discussion was informative and thought-provoking. The two most difficult social problems in Cuba then were alcoholism and unmarried women's pregnancies. In Cuba, no child is considered illegitimate. In both cases, there is much support and care given to the individual. In the case of alcoholics, if necessary they are sent away for treatment and then helped with a re-entry program.

The next topics were drugs and AIDS. At that time, there were fewer than 5,000 cases of AIDS throughout Havana. Drugs in Havana and other places were 5% or less of the population. Since the increase in tourism, these social problems have become worrisome, but are confronted early with education programs. The occupation of "social worker" was a newly-created position in Cuba.

DAY SEVEN

The weather in town was extremely hot. The worst memory I have of Trinidad is the flies. While having our lunch we were almost eaten alive by the flies. Because there were no windows in the restaurant, it was like their food swarming place. I was never so ready to leave a place in my life. At least on the streets, maybe I could be harder for the flies to find. There was a large restaurant in the hotel where we had most of our meals. Our meals there were well-prepared and tasty.

While in town, we visited the community stalls and did a little shopping. I bought a few items of lace and carved woods. There was not much variety from which we could select, but the people were so friendly and excited to see us that we enjoyed the venture. The homes were painted bright colors in shades of blues, deep and light yellows, pink, and built of material similar to stucco. These homes sat close to the sidewalks, allowing us to look straight into the houses. These homes reminded me of what was once called shotgun houses in America.

While in Trinidad we went to a community clinic and talked with a lady doctor. There are many doctors in Cuba. In this particular community, one doctor has180 patients, compared to doctors in the United States who have to see about 3,000 patients a year in an HMO (health maintenance organization). The doctors in Cuba are paid about $30 a month. Everything is provided for them by the government. The clinic was spotlessly clean but sparsely furnished. When we finished our visit and exited the clinic, there were only five or six patients waiting outside for treatment.

Cuba has an excellent health education program, using their radio announcements and printed information. They are always short on antibiotics and depend heavily on donations. When the doctor spoke of their education program, a rancher from Florida asked what I thought to be a very foolish question. He asked, with a typical American soft mind, "Oh, can they read?" I wondered whether or not he knew anything about why the revolution was fought and won. The illiteracy rate in Cuba is about 3% compared to 30-40% in some of the urban areas in the United States.

We spent two days in Trinidad—not long enough. We shopped, dined, and enjoyed the nightly entertainment in the amphitheater with the calm blue sea in the background. Every day when I awakened, the first thing I did was to look out at the sea.

On the way back, we traveled through the province of Cienfuegos, known as the "Beautiful City of the Sea." In 1560, the Spaniards settled there.

Day Eight

When I returned to our hotel, my room had been changed. I found it tastefully decorated and comfortable. I took a picture of the room and hung it on my wall back home. I call it "A Room in Cuba." During the day our electricity went out. When I first arrived, I had been told this sometimes happens. My room was on the third floor, so I wouldn't have far to walk up. The power was soon restored.

I enjoyed a wonderful afternoon buffet with the group, as thoughts of having to leave Cuba swarmed in my mind. There was a discussion with Evora about what would be our fondest and most exciting memory of the island. We agreed that the day we went on the search for the Cuban video and met the handsome French photographer, who was in Cuba for the Film Festival, was our most exciting memory.

His camera bag thrown over the shoulder of his soft, brown leather jacket, designer sun glasses complimenting his tanned face, and his silk shirt and slacks made him a rather dashing figure. He offered to help us find the video. Hailing a taxi, he said, "Please come with me. I will make sure I have you back in time to meet your group at the hotel."

Then Evora and I just looked at one another and nodded our heads, "Yes, thank you, thank you so much," as he hailed a cab for us. Everywhere we went there seemed to be beautiful ladies anxious to hug and kiss him. It was a fun day with this well-known personality in Cuba. We did find the video.

That night we had our farewell dinner at La Ferminia near the harbor and wall of the city. There was wonderful music and lots of dancing. We attended the "blasting of the cannon" after dinner. It was a night event with a solemn military ceremony and colonial-dressed soldiers marching to the beat of their drums on the way to prepare the cannon for firing. This was a re-enactment of a time in history when the towns-people were warned to get behind the wall before pirates and foreign ships would attack the city. This was done exactly at 9:00 each night.

We visited a few shops and then returned to our hotel. We would be leaving very early Saturday morning—at 5:30 a.m. During the night several of us became ill.

Day Nine

I had had no rest but no regrets when I arrived at the Havana airport with hundreds of people and long lines. I would have preferred the temperatures to have been a little warmer, with less rain in Havana during my visit. The weather is similar to the Florida climate with the feel of a subtropical environment. I was never disappointed with what I saw in this country or the group of people I traveled with. We were told that Cuba is the safest country in Latin America.

Thanks to the new friends I made (especially Evora Jordan, author and activist), and a special thanks to our excellent and helpful tour guide Roberto, a graduate of the University of Havana who helped make this trip a part of my continuing education and a wonderful friendship-building experience.

Roberto our tour guide. He had graduated from the
University of Havana, only because of the revolution.

I believed, and those beliefs were later confirmed, that
the people were healthy, employed and literate. There
was definitely the absence of ownership of property and
businesses after the revolution. Only a few family businesses
and farms were left in the hands of the original owners.
Years ago that started to change. Just recently it is reported
that the Cuban people now have home ownership. They are
allowed to sell and buy property. Recently I also read of all
the privately-owned businesses that are struggling because of
competition among them. Since Castro's brother Raul has
ruled, the country seems to be slowly progressing towards a
democracy.

Chao La Habana

Within less than an hour, our flight arrived in Miami. Then there was the grueling task of standing in long custom lines at the Miami International Airport, for longer than it took us to fly from Cuba.

Some custom officers were not happy that Americans had traveled to Cuba—asking in a crass manner, why I wanted to visit Cuba. What right did he have to question my motives? Don't I live in a democracy?

When I finally arrived at my hotel in Miami, I immediately went to bed. The plan was to meet with my friend Mara from South America, whom I hadn't seen in many years. She was in Florida doing post-graduate work for her doctorate. When she arrived, I just couldn't get out of bed because I was still suffering from the lack of rest and a stomach ailment. She was also tired and so we just enjoyed staying in our room and reminiscing—catching up on our lives.

The next day was Sunday and we did some sight-seeing and had a great dinner. We took a long walk on the beach the next morning, enjoying the sounds of the low tide and soaking up the warm sunshine. My visit to Cuba and reuniting with a long-time friend will forever be an abounding and grateful part of my life journey.

CONCLUSION

Americans have been forbidden from legally traveling to Cuba for seven-and-a-half years. Now, American citizens can go to Cuba without restrictions because the Obama administration has reauthorized the "People to People" trips, according to an article that appeared in the *Indianapolis Star* on August 11, 2011.

The moratorium on our travel to Cuba occurred after my trip to Cuba in December 2003. When I traveled there, it was under a "Letter of Authorization" licensed for education by *Insight Cuba—Cross Cultural Solutions*. Now you can travel under a specific license for "people to people" which is similar to the licenses that were provided from 1999 to 2003, according to *KGO Travel With John Hamilton*. Chartered air flights are allowed only from within Florida and, for a 45-minute flight, they are quite expensive.

Some citizens from the United States government do not want to see the rules loosening because that would encourage mass tourism to Cuba, according to what I have read. It's about economics—our money not flowing to Cuba through tourism and American business investments and trade. From other reports I've learned there are a few American businesses in the farming industry that are allowed to quietly conduct business with Cuba, but I am sure with many restrictions—still, through their connections, they slip through. Well, I say—good to the people of Cuba. This embargo has done nothing but hurt the innocent. The Cuban people suffer because of the shortage of antibiotics, and America's refusal to allow the export of catheters and other medical treatments. "Is the United States not guilty of the act of genocide?" one news article asked.

After working as a certified substance abuse counselor for 17 years, I discovered some counseling methods worked better than others in raising awareness about behavior and starting young women down the path to self-sufficiency. I understood that I couldn't save every young woman I was responsible for, but I could incorporate into their recovery plan a set of values for personal development and growth I hoped would reveal itself in their future. The following poem expresses my feelings about the successful efforts of one young lady to heal and change her life.

YOU HAVE RISEN

You have risen from
Low self-esteem to pride
Guilt to forgiveness
Anger to calm
Harsh to pleasant.
You have risen from
No boundaries to setting boundaries
Fear to courage
Hopelessness to hope
Dependent to independent.
You have risen from
Self-hate to self-love
Ignorance to knowledge
Dark to light
Immaturity to maturity.
You have risen from
Sadness to joy
Weak to powerful
Impatient to patient.
Who am I, to whom I have become
And
You are the witness.
You have risen.

In 1989, I was hired to work part-time as a substance abuse counselor for the Solid Foundation Mandela House Programs. I also became their volunteer fundraiser. This event was one of four that I chaired. We were honoring several well-known Bay Area citizens who were long-time supporters of the Solid Foundation. Minnie Thomas, the founder and executive director, opened her doors in 1987 to women addicted to drugs and alcohol.

OPENING REMARKS

G ood evening, Honorable Mayor Eilih Harris, Mr. Danny Glover, Reverend Cecil Williams, Madam Director Minnie Thomas, distinguished guests and staff. Welcome to our *Third Annual Benefit and Awards Ceremony*. On behalf of the Solid Foundation, I would like to express our deep appreciation to all our wonderful supporters who are here this evening and to those who could not be present—thank you for the extra effort you took to make this evening a success. We hope you will continue to feel the same enthusiasm next year and the next.

We've come a long way since our first benefit and awards ceremony in December of 1991. We are now able to put our own roof over our heads tonight. (Smile) This large portable tent we are in was set up for 300 people by Scott's of Jack London Square in Oakland, California.

Again this year, we have overcome our difficulties and struggles by surviving a budget cut, and have had tremendous success because of the goodness and charity of so many in the community. We cannot implement our programs and meet our goals without the help we receive from devoted staff, supporters and volunteers. There are thousands of others in this city who give so generously of their time to many worthy causes. There is an old African proverb that says, "It takes a village to raise a child." Now, it takes a whole community to raise a child and help a family.

In different ways we provide this tapestry of social fabric all over this city. This year Oakland received the prestigious "The All American City" because of people like you and thousands of others. Not because of any fancy downtown development or tall buildings going up, but because of the concern and generosity of its people.

Of all the places and in all the ways you spend your money, right here you get the biggest bang for your buck. No, the buck doesn't stop here because it keeps right on circulating through every generation to come. Therefore, you will get it back. It will come back to your communities and your streets.

Our theme this year, *"For the Good of the Child,"* exemplifies all we try to do here at the foundation, along with your help for the mothers in our program. We teach them how to get off welfare and rise to economic independence, and keep their families together.

No, we don't win all our battles. But then, who does? The equation will always remain two-sided, the win side and the lose side. But the ones we do win can make all the difference in the lives of the women and their children at the *Solid Foundation.*

All the grass-roots people in this country need to approach this life-threatening social problem with a simultaneous focus. We certainly don't have all the answers to problems in our communities and in this country, but we need to start asking some deep and serious questions about how we can stop the morbidity and mortality which has entrenched itself in our communities.

Though education and intervention, programs like the Solid Foundation touch lives and even save lives, but the pendulum is supposed to swing both ways, and as long as it doesn't, we'll never know what time it is. When are we going to focus on swinging it both ways? When are we going to demand that drugs are regulated and controlled and crime for profit removed? When are we going to start asking some hard questions of our lawmakers and government officials?

There is an old Negro spiritual with the words, "Oh Lord, it's too high to get over, Oh Lord, it's too wide to get around, Oh Lord, it's too low to get under." Does this begin to describe the problems in our communities?

Susan Taylor of Essence Magazine (one of our supporters), said, "Unmitigated greed and people in power without vision, compassion or plain good sense are fueling madness in our world."

We must all continue to stay together and work together. Can we always keep a roof over our heads and remember why we were here tonight? I can tell you how we all got here, because of a woman named Minnie Thomas, founder and executive director, who had a vision.

Where is your vision?

May the coming holidays surround you and your families with blessings and peace.

Thank you and we hope this evening will be enjoyable.

Benefit and Awards Ceremony
December 3, 1993
Oakland, CA

Carol L. Evans and Danny Glover.

THE ROSES: A GARDEN OF SECRETS

The scruffy appearance and the slow disappearance of the roses were the first visible sign that April's life was changing—that something she used to have was no longer there. It was like existing with a withered spirit and a weakened belief in her abilities. The secret of the rose garden could be found in the chaos of her life.

Flowering rose shrubs framed the corner lot of a deeply manicured lawn. The huge weeping willow tree, with its long green cascading branches, sat peacefully by, providing shade for their bedroom window. They were greeted by this incredible beauty each day of their departure and return. April felt accomplished looking at the stunning roses in her garden. And the house-dwellers felt protected by hundreds of little thrones precariously perched on the rose stems. Yes, life had given this family some of the very best—loyal friends, rich experiences and the ability to pursue their dreams.

Many neighbors and strangers admired and enjoyed the rose garden. The roses were something April took for granted would always be there, for her pleasure and others. They were planted tens of years before. Why shouldn't they be there for the rest of her life?

April had read that the yellow, red and pink China and Double Delight roses are hybrid teas. The roses were sometimes named after royalty, presidents and entertainment celebrities. Amazingly enough, there is something called "Rose" in mathematics. It is an equation formulated from the curve of the roses.

It had always been Brad's love of the roses that kept him caring for them. They constantly received his full attention—even above the sound of April's voice. His roses were always the pride of their neighborhood. This corner lot introduced the admirer of the roses to the neighborhood, home, and family. They were also his refuge from parts of his life he found unpleasant and uncomfortable.

One day, they received an envelope in the mail that was addressed "Neighbors" and a note saying, "Thank you for keeping your yard so beautiful. I love the roses." Placed inside, with the unsigned note, was a photograph taken of the roses.

What a kind gesture and thank you—for all the hard work and attention he gave to his roses. He took his bow and proudly accepted the credit for their beauty.

Often, April would find lovely bouquets throughout the house and always by the bedside. They spoke of a life moment—roses warming the spirit, comforting the soul and romancing the heart. Sometimes, she felt that the source of all her happiness came from their beauty, fragrance, and joy they brought to their home. She could not have known how fleeting and abstract her happiness was.

An opportunity for a productive outcome beyond the roses just didn't exist because a conversation other than the roses was only accusatory and angry. They didn't have the courage to have a broader and more realistic discussion about their lives. They needed a healing process or a treatment like the roses often received. The old dead undergrowth was not attended to in their lives. April often remembered lines from a poem she had read by Margie Driver.

> *A rose can say I love you and want you to be mine.*
> *A rose can say farewell when someone goes away.*
> *No matter what there is to say, a rose can say it best.*

The summer of 1985 unveiled a bitter-sweet reality of April's life with all its complexities. The bitter was soon to be the separation from her husband Brad, and the sweet was their son's departure for college. April was beginning to feel like lines from Thomas Moore's poem—"Last Rose of Summer."

> *All her lovely companions*
> *Are faded and gone.*

This tiny unit would soon be difficult to recognize as a family. So, she had to perform like her flowering shrubs, at the height of their season. She was the only one to attend to the affairs of the family, garden and home. One day, April realized, she must find the desire and strength to bring the roses back in the home—even to her bedside. The care-keeper of the roses discovered he wanted more from life. He saw no future in continuing his efforts to keep the roses beautiful. Years after Brad's departure her sadness would wane, and she would sometimes continue experiencing his kind deeds.

The last rose, no longer surrounded by all its familiar beauty, appears weak and forgotten. Strength was in their numbers and also in their beauty.

When they started losing their delicate petals, April had no desire to approach the roses; she found it too painful because the sense of loss was all around her.

After weeks and weeks, months and months of hoping she was still protected and loved, the roses began to disappear, and April no longer could pretend she had the strength or motivation to attend to the feeding, spraying and trimming that would yield the lovely roses for the next season.

It was now two years later—1987—when April started the painful and measured task of turning over the beautiful roses to the new inhabitants. Those two years with the roses was a struggle for the both of them. They quietly fought to survive on their own, just as she had. The huge weeping willow tree had died from within its trunk. One windy night it just uprooted itself and keeled over onto the road. April cried for hours at the loss of this beautiful tree. She thought—what else would she lose?

One day it was as if every thorn was suddenly attacking, and the pain was almost unbearable. April continued to feel pain from the rose thorn of life, long after being separated from her beautiful Rose Land.

After her departure, April never could have imagined the roses would have their life forever taken from their hallowed place at the hands of a stranger and nonbeliever. This was nothing less than desecration. But the spirit of the roses lived on in her heart and in her body art—one single rose.

Life without the roses forced April to feel stronger than ever about reality, truth, honesty, and responsibility. Life since the roses had shown growth and an understanding for forgiveness. Life since the roses had reacquainted her with her son and contributed to her spiritual growth. Her life after the roses was a life of giving, understanding and enjoying her life journey. The roses had taught her to awake each morning with a purpose in life, and make new discoveries about herself and others.

She enjoyed reaching out to her son and being a part of his dreams; this for April was now the most important part of her existence, each day. Her son was the best example of how she nurtured and protected what was most important in her life.

The rose garden now stood as her testimony of what had come and gone. April stopped searching and feeling sad about the diamond lost from her wedding ring in their rose garden. She no longer hated the ugly stump left by the death of her weeping willow tree. She just looked towards her future.

It was now a much simpler way of life—finding joy in having good health, a loving family, wonderful friends, and remembering with a smile how beautiful the roses were. And she appreciated whenever they were able to reach-out to each other—the father, his son and her child.

1938

April's birth, the debut of supermarket carts
The ballpoint pen
Superman
Instant coffees
Teflon
And Bob Hope's theme song
'Thanks for the Memories

WILLIE

William Franklin Evans, also known as Willie, is my father. He was a tall, handsome man with keen features. His fine black hair and his attractively-groomed mustache complemented his copper-color complexion. He spoke with a soft voice, always accompanied with a smile, unless you happened to be unaware of his short patience with shameless dishonesty, disloyalty or irresponsibility—then you found yourself at the chilly end of his moral polar.

He was born in Rome, Georgia, and moved to Indianapolis as a child. I hardly remember my paternal grandmother, and I believe his father died before I was born.

Mom and Dad were married on March 4, 1937 in Marion, Indiana and divorced when my sister and I were very young. They remarried on January 29, 1942 and once again divorced. I was born from the first marriage union and my sister Sandra from the second.

I don't remember much about my father until years after my mother and he had divorced. I never remember my mother having anything nice to say about my father. There was just a lot of anger and blame towards him accusing him of being a "lady's man."

Both parents had remarried by the time I was about twelve. Dad settled down and soon became a small-business owner along with his new wife, and he invited my sister and me to come and visit him whenever we wanted.

It was easy for me to make that decision for myself, being the oldest and probably the most curious about my father. I never paid much attention to my mother's complaints about him because I was always one to make up my own mind about how I felt. So off I went, almost every weekend, to visit my new family. There was a step-sister, a little older than myself with whom I got along with very well.

We were given three dollars a week allowance. It was so much fun catching the city bus and riding every Saturday to *Woolworths Five and Dime Store* and returning with a shopping bag full of goodies.

I developed a very healthy and loving relationship with my father until the day he passed. At the time he passed, I was married and living in California. But all the years before I left, we had become very close, from my childhood into my adulthood. I often confided in him and he was even acquainted with some of my friends. He was friendly and kind.

Once I became a young adult, I would help out in the liquor store my father owned. When I was not legally allowed in the store, I would sit in the office and storage area, doing what I could to help out. He also owned the restaurant next door and a night club.

I guess the most interesting thing about my dad was that he was a Republican. For several years Dad had worked as precinct committeeman. He felt that he was a successful businessman because he was willing to work hard and take advantage of all opportunities, and I agreed. He never had empathy for those who didn't have his values, and always commented that they were just lazy. He became friends with one of the most powerful politicians in the city during the 40's and 50's. My Dad told me the story of how the politician assisted him in getting his packaged liquor license in the Fifties.

Dad certainly had his faults, and I could always depend on my mother to point that out. I was so excited about their finally having a conversation on the phone. My Dad called, just as he promised he would, but then mother blew it! The conversation was short and unpleasant. The reason he had called was because I had asked him to. I had wanted a car for graduation and Dad was respectful enough to want to get my mother's permission before doing that. Well . . . . her answer was no, and he kept his promise to her. I was very angry with my mother and just thought it was all about not honoring my father and my wishes.

I just gave up on mother agreeing to anything my Dad wanted. I never again shared anything with my mother about my relationship with my Dad. She was who she was going to be and my relationship with my father was our private business. I respected him so much because he never, ever, had an unpleasant word to utter about my Mom.

There was a strange occurrence that seldom is a factor in families. It had to do with my father's next marriage after my stepmother passed from a rare blood disease. One day while I was visiting my Dad in the store, he said, "Carol, I have something to tell you. I'm getting married again."

After I got over the shock, I said, "Getting married again?"

I had not known my Dad to be interested in anyone since the death of his wife. All he did was work.

"Who are you marrying, Dad?

"I'm marrying Esther."

"Esther! You mean my step-sister . . . . your step-daughter?"

Then there was just silence for a very long time. I thought I was going to cry. Then so much anger and hurt suddenly occurred inside me. "I asked, "Why?"

He said, "Carol, before Martha passed she asked me to always take care of her elderly mother and she wanted me to marry Esther, her daughter."

At that time Esther was probably in her late twenties. She was a quiet and docile individual. I described her as old-fashioned and plain, but not now. She and I had grown apart years before. I found we no longer had anything in common. She was always polite and pleasant to be around. She never did anything to disrespect me—maybe, until now. She was just Esther and always around to work in the store. My grandmother used to say, "Still water runs deep."

I wondered why Esther never had a life of her own. She was completely devoted to her mother and grandmother, and I soon found out how devoted she was to my father. She always acted as if there was nothing out there in the world she seemed to be interested in.

Esther's mother wanted to make sure what she and my father had worked hard for would remain in her family, with her daughter and mother, at whatever cost. The businesses and any money would be kept out of the hands of another wife or his children. All I thought about was how deeply disturbing this all was to my psyche.

It took some time before I felt comfortable around my father and truly learn to forgive, but it was even harder to forgive Esther for this shameful and embarrassing arrangement. Time and time again I asked myself, was this marriage really approached as a business arrangement, or was it more than that?

My father passed in 1976 and my only other disappointment was that he never took time away from his business to come and visit me and my family in California, but I never doubted that he loved both his daughters. I had stopped judging Dad and Esther many years before his death, and learned to forgive and forget what some folks saw as the unspeakable sin.

Years later, taking my maiden name back gave me a new surge of courage and confidence—the confidence I was in need of. In my mind, it also honored my father's memory.

Our father William F. Evans
1910-1976

A SAILBOAT NAMED
SUMMARY JUDGMENT

W hat a day it had been. Clear blue skies, calm waters, and sailing with my friend in the Oakland Harbor. There was great conversation, fine wines, good appetizers and loud revelry on the high seas.

It was Sunday morning when I received a phone call from my neighbor and friend inviting me to sail with her and a few other guests on her new sailboat. She had received the boat as payment for a legal settlement from one of her clients.

I arrived at the docks along with others who were gathering for our outing. It seemed to be a friendly bunch of folks.

I was very impressed when I saw the beautiful white sailboat with its three colorful sails. This thirty-seven-foot sailboat could comfortably hold ten or twelve passengers. It had large windows inside the dining saloon allowing for lots of natural light. The teakwood-trimmed tables had matching seats that slid in and out. There was a well-equipped and small compact kitchen area with a wine cabinet. The bathroom was conveniently located on the bottom level of the boat, near the master bedroom.

My friend, an attorney for many years, had numerous stories to tell about her experiences in her legal practice. I certainly wanted to hear the story about this acquisition.

I wanted to remember, before leaving the boat, to ask my friend what was a "summary judgment." I knew this legal term had to be of great significance for this beautiful sailboat to have this name. I was anxious to learn the story about what this legal term meant to an attorney.

We left before noon. The weather was perfect for sailing—azure sky and warm sunshine. Even the Goodrich blimp was overhead. Along with the sailing trip, I was told we would stop at one of the many restaurants along the waterfront for dinner.

So many times I sat in the harbor watching families and lovers sailing and wishing I could do the same. However; I would just dream and try to imagine what fun they were having, while I continued to read my book, enjoy my cold drink, and soak up the warm sun.

More than a year before this lovely day, I had filed a lawsuit against my employer and soon my case would be heard in court. This day on my friend's sailboat was a day for relaxation and fun, to forget this weight on my shoulders. I would be expecting a call any day from my attorney.

It had been a year of anxiety, suspicion, suspense, and a year of great sacrifice and pain for me. I sometimes questioned and doubted my own faith about going down this road of going forward with the lawsuit against my employer, but I felt that there was no turning back.

During the procedure, I had been moved around to several different departments until we reached some kind of settlement. I was demoted in responsibilities, but not in pay. The attorney and I were waiting for notice of our court date. More than anything, I wanted my day in court to testify about the egregious methods used to avoid promoting me.

Now it was time to be in the moment and I was enjoying all the great conversations that ran the gamut of California experiences and professional life. They were a really friendly group of people. Thank goodness—no snobs.

It was near the dinner hour, so the conversations had turned to hunger and food, which could be heard throughout the sailboat. We all decided on Mexican food and this particular restaurant was known for its great margaritas.

We were nearing the pier, so it was time to begin picking up and placing items in fasten-down positions before arriving. I decided I would leave my large tote bag and only take a small purse. Then one by one we carefully stepped off the sailboat. We could smell all the wonderful food aromas as we walked up the path beside the restaurant, and hear the exciting, hip-shaking Mexican music.

After a couple of hours of enjoying our evening dinner, we headed back down the pier to our sailboat. I resisted thinking about how soon this perfect day would have to end, and then back to Monday morning life and the strain of wondering and waiting for what I called "justice."

I stepped cautiously from the pier onto the sailboat. We started our approach into the Oakland Bay. Sounds of classical jazz, softly playing, could be heard from where I sat outside on the deck, dreamingly staring out over the rippling waters.

The sailboat stopped, and then bumped a couple of times against the pier, suddenly jarring me into reality. Our captain stepped out to anchor and tie the sailboat.

After disembarking, we said our goodbyes and then left for the parking lot. I stopped and had a brief conversation with my friend about how much I enjoyed this Sunday outing and thanked her.

As we all drove away, I suddenly remembered I hadn't asked the one important question . . . . What was a *summary judgment?*

After a few days back on the job, my phone rang and it was my attorney. "Hello, Carol."

Nervously holding the phone, I said, "Hello, Mark."

"Carol, I'm afraid I have bad news for you."

I looked around to see if any staff was nearby. "What is it, Mark?" I asked.

"Carol, the judge has issued a 'summary judgment' in your case."

"What? A summary judgment?" I exclaimed.

After a long silence, Mark shouted into the phone, "Hello, hello Carol."

I no longer heard his voice as my thoughts drifted back to the sailboat, where those large black letters were painted on the side.

Suddenly I opened my eyes, my heart thumping, "Yes, Mark, yes."

I sat very still nervously tightening my hand around the phone receiver.

Mark started explaining what this all meant to my case: A *summary judgment* is when the judge becomes the "judge and jury" and examines all the legal documents in the case, from both sides and decides that one side hasn't proved their case. Then the judge refuses to hear that case in court.

Well, it was our side that the judge ruled against, and Mark needed to know what I wanted to do. My choices were to continue with the case or drop my case. The only choice I wanted was to win, but limited finances and abundant wisdom persuaded me that now was the time to retreat, because sometimes losing means winning.

You deal with life the way it is and not the way you want it to be.

That sailboat outing on *Summary Judgment* was a mysterious message that revealed itself at the right possible time, becoming a thundering and revealing life moment.

I never regretted my decision because a few years later a fair settlement was reached. I then embarked on a journey of self-confidence and defined my life on my own terms.

Legal definition of Summary Judgment: A decision made on the basis of statements and evidence presented for the record without a trial. It is used when there is no dispute as to the facts of the cause, and one party is entitled to judgment as a matter of law. (Source: www.USLegal. com)

THE RENEWAL

T he year was 1985. Ronald Reagan was president, *We Are the World* was recorded, *The Color Purple* was a movie blockbuster and gasoline was $1.09 a gallon. I was facing many challenges that would determine what kind of person I was. I had issues of abandonment and, most of all, fighting back thoughts of guilt and helplessness in my personal life.

I found that all the things I thought I had and loved were either disappearing or given to others, like certain job responsibilities in my office. For these reasons, I was losing hope. It was difficult to understand my feelings of helplessness and defeat. My painful and frightening emotions were masked by continued hard work and remaining active in my community, which afforded me balance in my life.

I had accepted the fact that I was not the person I used to be, because I no longer could breeze through my day without feeling like I was grieving for something lost. I didn't laugh as much, had fewer smiles and a less-positive outlook about life. It was as if I had been put into a time capsule that would be opened many years in the future when things would be better. I didn't know then, but now I know, I was also plagued by low self-esteem.

One day a note came across my desk from the college's assistant to the president. It was a request for the percentage of classroom usage at the college. This information would be included in the proposal for a new, five-million-dollar library to be built on the campus. I delivered this note to my supervisor, the registrar, and then watched the expression on her face.

I couldn't help but wonder how all this would turn out, since our statistician was on vacation and there was no one skilled enough in math to produce that information, not even our registrar. She was the least skilled and depended on us to do most of her work. She could only be described as incapable at performing many of her responsibilities.

Shortly after delivery of the request, I walked into my office to find my supervisor peering at the classroom assignment visual board I had ordered and designed, to update how the classrooms were allocated to professors. The antiquated way this process had been implemented for years was finally providing instant and precise information for the viewer.

She looked up and down, her head bobbing like a little bird. She was a pale, scrawny woman with short, carrot-colored hair. She would start to write on her pad, then appear defeated. She knew the answer to the percentage of classroom usage could be found on this display board. I continued to ignore her agonizing efforts to find the answer.

Hours later my moral conscious began to get the best of me. I thought maybe I should try and rise above whatever resentment I had for this lady and just remember how much I loved the college, from which I had received such a wonderful education. I had been taught important leadership skills, how to compete with my male counterparts, how to arrive at the right conclusions or solutions by considering both sides, how excited we all were about having a new library. Where was that person now?

I had no idea how to form a math equation that would produce the answer we needed. I just knew something had to be done to save our reputation around the college and, at the same time, maybe save her head. "Katie, can I ask what it is you are trying to do?" She replied, "Here's this note I received asking for classroom percentage use."

"Katie, would you like me to take a try at it?" I asked.

What was I saying? I must be out of my mind, I thought. I don't know a damn thing about math equations. I don't know what I'm talking about. Don't make a fool of yourself, Carol.

"Could I see what you have written down?" I asked with some trepidation. She handed me her note pad and then hastily removed herself from an uncomfortable position.

"I'll take a look at this and see what I can do with it," I said. She thanked me and quickly walked away, disappearing into her office. Now, what in the hell am I supposed to be doing on this hot seat?

As I sat contemplating how I would tackle this monster, I felt confident and determined to find the answer. (Where this confidence came from, I do not know.) My approach was first analytical by integrating all the elements. The information on the board had to be segregated and then applied to counts, rooms, and segments of time in a school day. Was this the right approach? Maybe it was. I had less than two working days to provide the president's office with my answer. For the next 14 or 15 hours I worked feverishly crunching numbers. I knew my answer had to be flawless and then explained to top-level staff in the president's office.

I found myself exhausted after the eighth or tenth time reading over my list of notes from the yellow pad on my desk. Each time I identified an element of the formula, I wrote it down. When I finished, there were seven steps that allowed me to arrive at the percentage of classroom usage. This was nothing short of a miracle. The next day, I walked into my supervisor's office and announced I had determined the figure was 87.2 percent. Her face glowed with relief and then, with a forced smile, she hung her head and thanked me. A moment of embarrassment for her turned out to be a lifetime of renewal for me.

By the afternoon of the day I finished going over my presentation, I was notified that I should be prepared to explain my principle to the president's office. One by one, they came in, and I was prepared each time to offer a clear and concise explanation for my work. There was only one challenger and I was able to disprove his theory. I just wanted to have this all over with so I could get back to my normal routine.

A few days passed. My supervisor walked in and dropped a worn, dark grey, hardcover book on my desk. She didn't say anything to me. For a moment I just stared at the book title, wondering why she gave it to me, and then where did it come from? I slowly picked it up and the title was "College Policy." *Hmm, I thought.* I opened the book and saw that it had been published in 1936, two years before I was born. On the other hand, how could I have ever known that something lying within the pages of this book would forever change the way I perceived how powerful the human mind is? Now I understand how little we know about using our minds.

I started reading the index of the book and found a chapter entitled "Find the Percentage of Classroom Usage." My first thought was to wonder why this book had not been used by someone to find this information the college needed, and why had I been put through all that stress?

Slowly I turned the pages, fearing everything I had done would be undone by this chapter in the book. I started reading and there staring at me was a seven-step solution—not eight or nine steps, but seven. As I read, each step was as exactly as I had written them on my yellow lined pad. Over and over again I read those steps in disbelief of what I had done. I asked myself, how did I know them? I had never seen this book before, or ever had any discussion about "percentage of classroom usage." This was all so mystifying and unbelievable to my ordinary way of thinking.

I closed the book and gave it back to my supervisor without either of us speaking a word. I'm sure some of the administration people had convinced themselves, I must have been privy to this book at some time. I had no earthly explanation and neither did they. All I knew was that something metaphysical had taken place. I have stopped trying to figure it all out and just accepted what I was able to do. Somehow I had been imbued with that information from the book—maybe from the time I was born, for this place in time.

This was the "renewal." From that day on, my life was never in need of being uplifted again. There was never again a struggle with my self-esteem. My confidence soared and my thinking became clearer than ever. For many years I didn't think about this "beyond my mind" experience. When I did, I just had to assume something special took place on those two days of my life. There are many unexplained secrets of the brain. Was my renewal experience one of them?

A PERSONAL NOTE TO MRS. CORETTA SCOTT KING

Dear Mrs. King,

Today I am extremely pleased and deeply honored to write, in your special book, a few simple words of love and praise to honor your memory.

It was in Oakland, California, where I had the opportunity to meet you. I so vividly remember how beautiful you were, what a lovely smile you had, and how I felt your spiritual energy.

I once heard you speak and I knew then how special you are. I am so grateful for this experience and my special memories of you. You have touched so many hearts and inspired so many minds. I am especially honored to discover I was born on your birthday, April 27th.

C. L. Evans

This poem is dedicated to my mother, Jean C. Lindsay Evans Williams Tate. She was a woman who loved life so much she gave her entire heart and every conscious moment to inhaling sometimes too deeply, breathing too shallow, and then realizing the reality sometimes came too harsh and swift. She never met a stranger, and her smile and laughter was unforgettable. She was impetuous and stubborn and caring and loving. As a young girl she was noticed by her teachers to be bright and talented. She studied hard and did well in school. For many years she was given piano lessons, in which she excelled. Then life 'just got in the way.' Life took so much of her away from so many of those beautiful feelings about her early years. It was the loss of her music that I want to remember. So I have written a poem expressing how I feel about remembering my mother's music.

MAMA, WON'T YOU PLAY FOR ME JUST ONE MORE TIME?

You told me how you learned to play in your home town
I haven't heard you play since I was a small child
Back then, it just was not enough for tiny ears to hear
The sound of your music, I barely remember those years
Mama, won't you play for me—just one more time

Nobody knows any more the music you played for me
Few family even know, and others can't recall
That music was part of your life, years long before
I knew that it was taught to you, all your young life
Mama, won't you play for me—just one more time

I never saw enough of you on that piano stool
You were the master over those ivory keys
You learned to play Bach, Beethoven and Chopin
This should never be forgotten or lost from our mind
Mama, won't you play for me—just one more time

We know sometimes life gets in the way
And that's why you could not continue to play
Those who don't believe, who had never heard your music

Will be convinced by me, how well you touched those keys
Mama, won't you play for me—just one more time

The music you learned to play, so beautiful to be near
And you also mastered your studies during those years
Earned your membership in the National Honor Society
For all those who do not know, I have proof of that to show
Mama, won't you play for me—just one more time

Your music mattered so much you had it taught to us
We now understand how life sometimes gets in the way
Sadly enough, the music you loved so much stopped with us
But that is not a reason to forget—So . . . .

Mama, won't you play for me—just one more time?

Please Mama, please!

Jean Lindsay Evans

A CHARMING LIFE

*T*he Rose, the Boston Skyline, the Shoe, the Canadian Leaf, the Angel, the Cape Cod Map, the Comb, the Statue of Liberty, my Zodiac Sign, the United States Capitol, the Boston Crab, and a Love Box are all hanging from my Charm Bracelet. These twelve charms bring back so many pleasant memories.

The *Rose* is my favorite flower and the title of one of my stories. My home was surrounded by hundreds of lovely roses admired and loved by my family, friends and the entire neighborhood. It wasn't difficult for me to make this purchase because of those lovely roses.

I love visiting the historic city of Boston, especially the Boston Harbor with all the famous seafood restaurants, the old Quincy Market, the ride through the city's cobblestone streets, and discovering old buildings and their past. While I was there, I enjoyed my favorite crab dinner and traveled by ferry over to Martha's Vineyard, where I found the *Cape Cod Map*.

Shoes are a woman's weakness, so I couldn't resist purchasing the *Shoe*. We must have every style and color. They are in boxes, in shoe bags, on shoe racks, stored in plastic containers, and under beds. When ladies visit the shoe department at Nordstrom's we are tantalized by all five of our senses, reducing our resistance to zero.

The *Statue of Liberty* is a great attraction where I once climbed to the very top without fear or hesitation.

My zodiac sign is *Taurus* and that was a charm I purchased because it represents an important part of my spirit.

I once visited our Capitol and saw the Senate in session. When I found the *U.S. Capitol Charm*, I recognized this building as the most important symbol of our democracy.

The *Canadian Leaf* is a reminder of my travels to Montreal and Quebec, two very different cities; one ultra-modern and the other in the French tradition.

The next two charms I will mention are my *Comb* and the *Angel*. This feminine and decorative comb caught my eye; a comb can perform many duties: for instance, holding the hair in place, changing the hair style, and it can be a symbol of beauty and charm.

I adore my *Angel Charm*. Angels are very special to me. I'm sure I have my own personal angel watching over me.

Last but not least is my special *Love Box* where a secret note can be placed when you unlatch and lift its tiny lid.

My life hangs by a charm.

THE TRAVELING HEART

Many years ago there was a middle-aged gentleman who was a magnificent writer. He became famous in his home town because everyone who knew him often heard the stories of love letters to a lady living far away.

Because of his superb knowledge of the English language, during his time in the military he had often received requests from the men in his unit to write love letters for them. These letters were mailed to their sweethearts. Jake was flattered and proud to be of assistance in helping love travel so far.

Jake Heart lived in the small town of Wasilla, Maine, where he worked at the post office for many years. Wasilla's population was 896. Its industries were fishing and tourism. During the summer its harbor was always a busy place, filled with small fishing boats, sailboats, and a few expensive yachts. During the summer months, the yachts were a beautiful sight to watch coming around the bend—in and out of the harbor. Some of the wealthier families sailed to Wasilla on their way to their summer homes. They would moor their boats and shop at the businesses along the wharf.

Jake would frequent the barber shops, cafes and the general store, telling his stories about the lady he loved so much, and hoping they would soon be together. Folks always asked him how many letters he had written in the past months, and if he and his lady friend would soon marry. Jake had never married and he was always teased by everyone about needing someone to cuddle up with during those cold winter nights in Maine. His only companion was a 15-year-old black and white cocker spaniel named Joe. Jake and Joe were a constant fixture on the streets of Wasilla and down by the harbor they loved so much.

Jake would always promise that his lady friend would visit soon, and then everyone would have a chance to meet her and see how beautiful and kind she was. But months and months and years and years went by. Jake's lady friend and love never arrived. Jake had often said she was afraid of flying, and the train or bus was such a long ride, so Jake often traveled to visit her.

Some of his friends noticed that Jake seemed to be having a few health challenges. They worried because he was alone and was not close to any of his relatives. One day while he was having his hair cut, his barber became concerned about how weak he seemed to be. Jake had never complained or mentioned any illness. He left the shop with old Joe and slowly made his way home.

Folks began to see less and less of Jake and his dog and, since he had retired from the post office, he was hardly ever seen except when he was mailing his love letters or doing a little shopping. Then one day neighbors noticed the ambulance, police and fire trucks in front of Jake's house. Neighbors watched while Jake was carried out and put into the ambulance. The next day, when his friends received the news of Jake's death, sadness and gloom quickly spread over the town.

A cousin arrived to handle the funeral arrangements. These were simple and short, just the way Jake wanted. While his cousin was going through his belongings, he found boxes of love letters that had never been opened. They were returned and stamped "person unknown." Could it be this was all a charade? Was this lovely woman created by Jake? Did she ever exist, except in his mind?

His cousin was mystified because he had heard Jake speak of his love so many times, and with such admiration and inner peace. As he shuffled through what seemed to be hundreds of love letters, he could not resist reading a few. There were phrases like, "I want to be your catalyst for peace of mind and your reinforcement for your inner well being." "You are wonderfully wonderful, and I consider myself to be a very blessed man, as I am enriched through knowing you."

Jake's cousin reached a compassionate decision. A small amount of his ashes and a few of the love letters would become a part of Jake's memorial service for the town. Five love letters were selected from a five-year span. They were placed in five jars, along with a portion of his ashes, and sealed.

Then Jake's cousin and many of the town folks walked slowly down to the harbor, carrying lighted candles. No words were spoken, just eyes focused out to the sea, with thoughts and many questions about Jake hanging heavily in the air. The bottles with ashes and love letters were tossed in the sea, along with hundreds of roses.

On this warm evening night, a full moon shines over rapidly moving sea waters. The bottles bob up and down, and then float out farther and farther until they can no longer be seen. Jake's traveling heart perhaps will reach a lovely lady who will appre*ciate* receiving a love letter.

HE

Revered by his father and unconditionally loved by his mother, his adult life was a continuous struggle for a place to be in the world. The early childhood years were wonderful and he still speaks of those days today. He grew up to be a young man interested in, and understanding the rewards of, success.

He had a small-built frame but enjoyed being competitive in sports such as track and skiing. Playing sports was one of the times his shyness disappeared; he displayed lots of excitement and courage, and he smiled and laughed a lot.

He was exposed to the better part of this society all through his formative years, teens and beyond. He always talked about the day when he would attend college. In his late teenage years he had gravitated towards his father's spoken thoughts and daily advice. He was slipping away from mother wisdom.

He was comfortable with his parents' values and beliefs, and he was an easy child to raise. He was kind, polite, gentle, and always attracted to friends who had the same values he had been taught.

He never was attracted to fads of the day or hanging out—just doing nothing. He had two or three close friends with whom he spent most of his hours outside of home and school. He was loyal and faithful to his friends, just as he was in other parts of his life.

He envisioned his American dream and his opportunity to contribute to his community. He was dedicated, devoted and determined to make a good life for himself. He was striving and reaching for a bright future. He saw success starting to trickle his way.

He felt obligated to please the male parent whom he viewed with the most intelligence and strengths. He sought his approval and could have had no way of knowing how, in the far future, that this parent would have a strong and harmful influence over his life. The deepest parts of him would someday struggle to be free—unsuccessfully.

He was clueless about his instability and paranoia for a long time. The approaching years of his illness left him frightened and confused. There were many demons for him to battle. His desires, dreams and plans gradually disappeared, leaving him hopeless, but not without a deadly and horrible exit.

REMEMBERING DELLA

DECEMBER 2, 2011

Della was an exuberant, charismatic, vivacious and thoughtful spirit. She was the living example of family love and friendship love. She was always meeting and greeting new faces and loving to make new friends, while remaining loyal and devoted to old friends.

The Nora Commons Creative Writing Workshop was a part of her life she enjoyed so much, along with many other activities at Nora Commons.

So it was on this path that we met this delightful and energetic lady who contributed so much to our learning experience. When Della wrote and read at our workshop, she took us on a great adventure or down memory lane—sometimes with reading props to highlight her story and engage our minds.

We are here today to share and reminisce about the journey she took with us, and now we will have to continue our journey without her.

Della will be long remembered in a cheerful and wonderful way by all of us.

With Loving Memories,

Members of the Creative Writing Workshop

YES, YOU CAN DEPEND ON ME

You can depend on me.
Yes, you can depend on me.
I will do my best to be the best.
Yes, you can depend on me.

Remember when I was not at my best—
Until I was given the chance to do my best.

Yes, you can depend on me.

I am contralto Marion Anderson, one of the   MUSIC
Greatest singers of the 20th Century and
The first African-American to perform
With the New York Metropolitan Opera.

Yes, you can depend on me.

I am Althea Gibson, the first African-American   SPORTS
To win a Wimbledon singleton title.

Yes, you can depend on me.

I am Dorothy L. Brown, the South's first   MEDICINE
African-American surgeon.

Yes, you can depend on me.

I'm Evelyn Fields, U.S. Navy lieutenant and   MILITARY
The first African-American woman to   SERVICE
Command a naval ship.

Yes, you can depend on me.

I am Sidney Poitier, the first African-American   ACTOR
To win the Oscar for Best Actor.

Yes, you can depend on me.

I am Thurgood Marshall, the first   JUDICIAL
African-American justice appointed to the
U.S. Supreme Court.

Yes, you can depend on me.

I am Mary McLeod Bethune, educator,   EDUCATOR
Civil rights leader, government official,
And chairperson for FDR's Federal Council
Of Negro Advisers, "Black Cabinet."

Yes, you can depend on me.

My name is Barack Hussein Obama,   COMMANDER
And I am the first African-American elected   IN
To be President of the United States of America.   CHIEF

And yes, you can depend on me.

DEAR RAYNA

February 9, 2011

Subject: Senior Retreat

Dear Rayna,

Words are very powerful and sometimes magical, whether written or spoken. As you arrive at your next juncture in life, I'm thinking about "words of encouragement" for my great-niece.

When you were a baby and tried to take your first steps, you had to fall and get up and fall and get up, again and again, finally walking and then running. You never gave up, did you?

I think of your life journey and what you will need to always carry with you; just like on any journey, you want to make sure that when you arrive at your destination, you have taken what you will need to carry you over and on—your values.

The first and foremost important value to carry with you is courage, because without courage your vision will die. The second most important value for your life's journey is patience. Patience is a virtue and it moves quietly to create and grow success.

I KNOW YOU WILL DO GREAT AND BE GREAT AT WHATEVER YOU WANT IN LIFE.

CONGRATULATIONS!

Love,
Aunt Carol

Aunt Carol at Rayna's high school graduation party in 2011.

THE BIG CHILL IS ON

Gone are the summer days—with all the colorful flower gardens and manicured lawns in a city of tree-lined streets. We certainly enjoyed our parks, swimming pools, outdoor entertainment and all the barbeques.

Sitting on balconies or benches under a balmy summer sun are no longer a part of our days, just a part of our memories . . . The big gray sky hovers over us. Orange, yellow and brown leaves float downward from the trees, turning them into dull brown, skeleton-like images. On the eve of winter, each day, darkness will come too soon—**The Big Chill Is On.**

We cannot forget to mention those bright summer moonlit nights that some of us managed to stay awake and catch sight of after the warm sunny days. Memories of the Monon Trail always cooled by thick green vegetation, intermingled with tall trees, will soon be abandoned by most of the outdoor types on bikes, skate boards, skaters and runners and walkers, followed by their pets. Groceries pulled in wire carts by the older folks, with a watchful eye, will require another method of transportation. There goes the summer—**The Big Chill Is On.**

If you exhausted a good part of a week lifting, tugging, emptying, replacing and hanging clothes—this was your big clothes shift from summer to winter—**The Big Chill Is On.** Soon, the thrill of managing to swivel, bump and swerve around potholes that need filling and uneven asphalt that needs resurfacing is a stark reminder of the winter season.

Now, our trips to the airports will require heavier luggage (more money for the airlines) stuffed with our long underwear, turtle necks, wool sweaters, wooly socks and cords. Unless you are lucky enough to travel to Florida, then you'll struggle with trying to peel off all the winter gear before boarding your flight. So—you're leaving **The Big Chill** and refusing to give up those warm summer days. Ugh—Snowbirds.

SEVENTY-FOUR SPRINGS

What a great way to look back at my life, counting in springs instead of years; not to mention that it gives me a fresh and clear sense about where I go from here by the seventy-fifth spring. For some reason, this doesn't sound quite as scary; it even puts me in good spirits.

Spring semester, spring break, spring has sprung; the month of my birth is April, along with April showers, tweeting of birds, arrival of tulips, daffodils, and the return of blossoming trees. I get to hibernate during those cold and gray times of the year and store up my strength. If I could only consume less food while I lie dormant, it wouldn't have to be "fat spring" in April.

Instead, I hibernate with all my kitchen gadgets. I have my state-of-the-art countertop oven, my juice maker and my food twister. I grill and bake with convection and infrared. I mix, chop and stir in my juice maker and twister. My excuse is—I will be an expert at preparing all these exotic dishes for my family and friends when spring arrives. I will be lauded for my culinary skills and sought after for party invitations.

The other side of spring is, of course, all the talk about spring cleaning. Spring requires us to clean-up and clean-out. So I labor in my storage area, searching for anything I can donate to Goodwill or sell at the Nora Commons spring sale. I try to stay focused and not meander all over and head off in other directions.

My last spring reflection is that of our antiquated tax system and the arrival of Mother Nature's crawly and creepy little creatures. I don't know which annoys me the most.

NORA COMMONS CREATIVE WRITING WORKSHOP

This week was 'Free Choice' for our weekly writing assignment. Once I pinned it down, I knew that no other subject could be more enthusiastically approached by me than the *Nora Commons Creative Writing Workshop.*

I have always believed that the most important thing for me to do during my life is to make sure I surround myself with people who contribute in a positive way to my mind and spirit. I have been inspired and educated by all of you. Our time on earth never stops revealing new and exciting life changes and growth, no matter what age we are.

So, out of respect and concern for each other's work, we become friendly critics and share a great learning experience while continuing to improve our writing skills.

I love the adage, "Knowledge is power, but enthusiasm pulls the switch." So, I keep my hand on the switch. No matter where I go, whom I meet, or what I learn, I'm very passionate about the wisdom that comes from all of you.

Every Tuesday, when I attend our workshop, a new seed is planted about how to improve my writing and everyday life. I truly believe we can't improve or do better unless we follow great examples of others. We have experienced a measure of shared learning that promises to be one of those defining moments—congratulating and celebrating one's accomplishments and success—our first book signing for our own eighty-three-years-young published novelist.

By coming together every week, each of us reminds the others that we all are created with a lifetime of potential. The experts say that during one's lifetime, we only use 1/4 of our potential. Well, we certainly are pushing on with a healthy and enthusiastic approach to the other 3/4.

So thanks to all of you for believing that together we can become better writers and better individuals. Write on!

THE LIEUTENANT
AND THE CORPORAL

How many times had I rushed to her side to help after her body had fallen to the floor, and then crazy with fear, wondering if this would be the time she would not be able to raise herself up and walk? Or the times I watched her shuffle slowly from one place to another, trying to walk? I didn't know about all the pain she was having in her legs.

Saturday morning of the Memorial Day weekend, May 28, 1973, I cuddled my darling sister's head in my arms while waiting for the ambulance to arrive. When she stood up and then leaned on the door frame and started to slide to the floor, I screamed for help from Rheena, the graduate student from India, who stayed with us. She came running and I asked her to call the police. I was on the floor of my TV room holding my sister Jean Ann's head in my arms. I listened closely to the last sound she ever made, and later remembered the first sound I ever heard her make as she was coming into the world. She was born at home on August 29, 1947.

I was almost ten years old when Jean Ann was born with her little body in need of surgery. I remember Mother telling the family how Jean Ann's appendix was twisted, and she would have to be operated on to correct this condition. As she grew up, she seemed to be healthy but she always had less energy. There were even times when she was thought of as just being lazy. She would sit and read books for hours every day, while the rest of us would complain about her not doing her share of the chores around the house.

Jean Ann had spent the Memorial Day weekend at my home because she was traveling with me, my husband, and my son to Carmel by the Sea. I remember her saying, "Oh, Carol, since I haven't gotten your birthday present, just pick something out in Carmel."

That weekend I kept a close watch over her because in my heart I felt so afraid—how much time did she have? How long could she live with this condition? I remember her grayish skin tone. This did not seem nor look normal.

Jean Ann was always generous and kind to everyone. I loved my baby sister very much, and was so troubled by what was going on with her health. I was frightened because I didn't know how I could help her. I had tried to convince her to move back with me and my family, but she had repeatedly refused.

Jean Ann had always been a very private person, not saying more than was necessary, so we could never tell what she was really feeling or thinking. This was seriously one of those times. She was keeping big secrets—always proclaiming everything was okay while she was seeing her doctor.

Jean Ann arrived in Oakland, California in the late summer of 1971. There was a knock at my door and when I answered, there was my baby sister. I was overcome by this surprise and I just wanted to throw my arms around her. She came in and sat down, and then commenced telling me how sorry she was that she hadn't called me about her plans to visit. The last time I had seen her was at Fort Riley, Kansas, where she was stationed, when we were driving across country on our way to California.

She had been in San Francisco for two days before making up her mind to permanently come to Oakland to live. I knew her assignment with the military had not ended, so I just didn't understand why she sounded so final about everything.

Jean Ann had graduated from Marian College in 1969 with a degree in history, and then immediately had gone into the military with a commission of first lieutenant. The Army had paid for her last two years of college and in return she would enlist with them for four years.

She continued her story, telling me she had driven straight through from Kansas and was no longer in the military. I was truly baffled and asked her to explain why. I knew she still had two years to serve. I got the biggest surprise of my life when Jean Ann confessed she was pregnant and was forced to resign from the military, with an honorable discharge. She started to cry and then we were both crying. I could just imagine how much shame and heartbreak she was suffering. Then, when I thought it couldn't get any worse, well, it did—the father of the baby was a married military officer. She said she had not known he was married, and I believed my sister because she was one of the most decent and honest individuals I knew.

We all stayed in a temporary home belonging to my brother-in-law while looking for a house to buy. I had decided not to question Jean Ann anymore, nor remind her about how wrong her life had gone. I would just do the best I could for her.

She was excited about our purchase of a new home and would live for a year with my family and me before getting out on her own.

The baby was due in about five months, and I wanted to do whatever I could to assist her. I soon learned that my sister had made a crucial and frightening decision—she said her baby would be adopted. Finally, I asked what must have been the most complicated question ever for her to answer. Why? There was no changing her mind.

We soon found a house, at a good price, that we all could be comfortable and happy with and it was in a well-established neighborhood. Jean Ann actually spotted it before I did. So by November of that year we moved in. It wasn't long before her baby was due. One day she came to me with a letter from our mother. The letter was in condemnation of her weakness and moral ineptness to remain unsoiled. And my baby sister spoke of how she struggled with the thought of killing herself, if she couldn't live with her embarrassment and the heartbreak she felt she had caused her family.

I was so troubled by our mother's pious letter; I immediately called her and registered a thundering disapproval of what she was doing to her own daughter. I angrily reminded her that we weren't living in heaven, but on earth-an-imperfect planet. She had just better start learning how to forgive, and continue to warp her arms around her daughter. Mother soon dropped her misguided beliefs and reached out with tenderness and love. I told her that we all had to get through this without stomping all over our personal feelings and beliefs in our family. Time takes care of everything we may think is ugly or beautiful in life if we have the right response.

I remember going to the Navy hospital where the Sisters of the Good Shepherd had made arrangements for Jean Ann's child to be adopted immediately after birth. I held him for just a moment. So much love and sadness invaded my body and my mind while looking at this beautifully formed baby boy. I couldn't feel anger, only sympathy, for my sister. What a frightening time for all of us.

For the next few months we busied ourselves with getting back to normal. Jean Ann found a job in San Francisco with an insurance company. We all loved the new home and I busied myself with decorating it. I also had just started a new job, and my son was in a new school.

That year went by so quickly. Jean Ann found an apartment near Lake Merritt in Oakland. I was happy for her but at the same time regretted her departure. Since I was ten years older, my sister and I had had very little opportunity to know each other as adults. I couldn't remember ever going to a movie or restaurant with my sister. Now I thought it would be wonderful to spend time together.

She was such a beautiful spirit to be around. She had a copper complexion with a large-boned frame, and was a little taller than her sisters. She wore glasses and had a very studious appearance. She was never into fashion like my sister and I. But her laugh and smile made her sparkle.

One day, while speaking to my sister on the phone, I suddenly heard a thump. There was no response when I called out to her. Then I heard her voice over the phone. I nervously asked her what had happened and she said she had fainted.

At that time a contagious flu virus was spreading throughout the country, causing grave consequences. People were fainting and suffering other effects of this flu, so when Jean Ann fainted I quickly contributed it to that flu virus. She soon confided in me that she had fainted twice in San Francisco—once in the cafeteria line at work and again on the street.

Jean Ann assured me she had seen a doctor and was having lab work done. Discovering all this bad news about my sister's health was very troubling. Then my worst nightmare came true—she progressively became worse and had to resign her job. I tried to convince her to give up her apartment and come back to live with me, but she wouldn't agree. She became weaker and weaker and continued to faint. Her doctor had put her on a blood thinner, but there was no cure for her pulmonary hypertension. Watching her struggle with everyday life left me with precious little hope. The condition was caused by restricted flow of the blood through blood vessels and arteries.

I think about how differently her life had been with her rank of corporal, then her life as the lieutenant. Not that I knew that much about her college life, because I lived out of the state, but I knew as a corporal and college student she had been eager and optimistic about life. Just like other college graduates, she looked forward to starting her career. As the lieutenant, she suffered her worst nightmares and then finally death.

When I spoke to her doctor that fatal day, she said that Jean Ann knew some day she would faint and just never recover. Of course, her doctor could not reveal this prognosis to me before my sister's death without her permission.

I grieved for so long for her and the nephew I would never know. I wondered where he was and who was his family? I wondered if he was happy and, when he grew up, would he want to know who his birth mother was? Would he ever want to find any of his mother's family? I never gave up hope that this could happen one day.

LITTLE GRANDMA
1886-1985

Effie Jane Stewart Lindsay was born in 1886, near Terre Haute, Indiana, on an Indian and Black settlement. She was the youngest of seven children and all her brothers and sisters died very young, as folks often did in those days. Her mother passed shortly after she was born. Effie was raised by her aunt in Champagne, Illinois.

Little Grandma's great-grandchildren lovingly called her by that name because in children's eyes appearance is important, and the difference in their two grandmas' heights made one appear "big" and the other "little." This adorable greeting always got their two maternal grandmothers' attention in a loving way.

The settlement of Lost Creek, northeast of Terre Haute in Vigo County, was where Blacks and Indians worked and lived side by side building a school, church, store and/or their homes, and everyone was kin to one another. This story was first told to me by my mother.

Important family lineages came from Lost Creek. The "quasi-free" Negroes started businesses, purchased land, had farm animals, and grew their food. They began settling from the South around 1830. This was an environment that nurtured dreams, encouraged accomplishment, and placed a high value on education and habits of hard work. One of the families had a son who grew up to be a special assistant to the Secretary of Agriculture under two Democrat U.S. presidents. [2]

It was rumored that Little Grandma's mother was Cherokee and her father was Caucasian. Little Grandma had high cheekbones, a reddish complexion and long back hair that hung to her waist. You could be fooled by her tiny frame and small stature of less than five feet because she could stand her ground with the most robust of them all. She had proved time and time again how tough and resilient she could be. I never witnessed fear in her eyes, yet she was tender, kind and loving to her grandchildren. They were her life.

Little Grandma's husband, Grandpa Lindsay, was the town barber in Lebanon, Indiana, where they lived for over 20 years. They married in 1912. She was his second wife and married him when she was only 18 and he was 45. His first wife had died and left three young children. He and my grandmother had two children—Jean and Wayne. My grandfather bought a home on South Evans Street in Lebanon and their children attended Lebanon High School.

Grandpa Lindsay was well known in Lebanon because many folks were customers at his barbershop. When the owner of the only department store in Lebanon would travel to New York to buy clothes for the next season, he would come in the barber shop and tell my Grandpa to have Effie, Jean and Wayne come in to his store and pick out whatever they wanted to wear. As a result of his kindness, the Lindsay family was one of the best dressed in town.

After my Grandpa Lindsay's death in 1936 (two years before I was born), Little Grandma sold the home and she and the children moved to Indianapolis. Mother always

---

[2] Historians: Robert Barrow and Lawrence D. Hogan

complained about Little Grandma selling their home and coming to Indianapolis instead of staying in Lebanon. She was also unhappy that Little Grandma either sold or gave away so many heirlooms and family memorabilia; but I understood because Little Grandma would often talk to me about her decision to sell the home and move to Indianapolis. She just couldn't endure the loneliness of her home after the death of her husband and then her two children leaving. She wanted to be closer to them and her grandchildren.

We all lived together, except for my sister Sandra, who lived with our elderly godparents. Mom and my stepfather had bought their first home when I was twelve. Little Grandma came to live with us. I was so happy because I loved Little Grandma very much!

I remember Little Grandma was totally dedicated to her grandchildren, while our parents worked. She cooked, cleaned and took care of us until the last child left home for college.

She had attended school through the seventh grade and could often help the grandchildren with their homework. Little Grandma loved to read those romance magazines of the 50s and 60s—*True Romance* and *Love Story*. I would just chuckle to myself whenever I saw her reading them, with a delightful smile that was perfectly formed around her toothless gums.

One day Little Grandma told my mother that she needed to buy a new girdle. The family had shared with her their plans to travel to California. Well, we knew that meant she was planning to travel with the family and fly for the first time, because Little Grandma didn't go anyplace without wearing her girdle. This was a serious decision, wanting a new girdle. We would also have the privilege of seeing her pearly-white dentures, which she never wore. How beautiful she looked! This was all for a trip to California to visit with my family and me, and we all traveled south to Mexico. I think that was the longest trip she had taken. Not many years later she had a stroke. She was in her nineties and had to be put in a nursing home.

Little Grandma had the jolliest laugh. When she laughed it was also her way of stating her approval of something she had just heard or seen. Then she would put her hand over her mouth and shake her head side to side, as if it was beyond her belief and seemed impossible.

When I was a little girl and snooping one day, I found some beautiful gold coins wrapped in tissue and stuck in the corner of a dresser drawer. I used to pull them out often and just admire them and then sneak them back. Of course, I didn't understand their value, nor did I understand they may have been illegal to have because President Roosevelt had taken this country off the gold standard in 1933.[3] I found these coins around 1950.

One day I wanted to look at the shiny gold coins, but I frantically searched and couldn't find them. I never asked about them because I was not supposed to know anything about them and their hiding place; but then, one day mother found out that Little Grandma had paid the news paperboy with the coins, when she didn't have enough change. Mother must have fussed and complained for months about what her mother had done. I was sad because the beautiful coins were forever gone from my eyesight.

Other memories of Little Grandma were those of wearing her shoes. Her small feet were only a size four and I enjoyed walking around in her shoes, which were prettier than mine. Today little girls' shoes are designed in the same styles as their mothers' shoes.

---

[3] Website: FDR takes United States off gold standard—History.Com

Little Grandma could walk so fast with her small feet and short legs. Whenever she took me places with her, I could hardly keep up and would always be out of breath by the time we walked back.

During my difficult teen-age years, Little Grandma would always be near to comfort and share her wisdom. She had a listening ear and plenty of patience for a young girl with growing inner struggles. She was my "rock."

A few weeks before she passed, I was visiting with her and as I leaned over her and whispered my expressions of love in her ear, with great effort she lifted her frail, trembling hand and stroked my cheek for the last time.

I just bet that the shot of whiskey she would sometimes take at night contributed to her longevity. She lived until she was 99 years old.

Every day of my life, I am filled with tender gratitude for her.

Uncle Wayne, our mother Jean and Effie Lindsay, our grandmother.

RECOMMENDED READING

Go, Tell Michelle: African American Women Write to the New First Lady
Compiled and Edited by Barbara A. Seals Nevergold and Peggy Brooks-Bertram
State University of New York Press, Albany, 2009

Crazy:
A Father's Search Through America's Mental Health Madness
Pete Earley
Berkley Books, New York, 2006

The Emotional Incest Syndrome: What to Do When a Parent's Love Rules Your Life
Dr. Patricia Love with Jo Robinson
A Bantam Book, New York, 1990

Cuba:
Ediciones Niocia S.L.
Legal dep.:B-46168-2002

Death of a Revolutionary: Che Guevara's Last Mission
Richard L. Harris
W.W. Norton & Company, Inc., New York, 2002

ABOUT THE AUTHOR

Carol L. Evans is the oldest of five children. A native of Indianapolis, Indiana, she moved in 1971 to Oakland, California, where she was employed by Mills College, and also earned her bachelor of arts degree in sociology prior to retiring in 1994. In addition to publishing the annual Positive Images of Oakland Calendar for ten years, Ms. Evans also wrote the award-winning short story *Katrina: The Ghosts of 1865* and numerous other stories that were published in four senior anthologies. A contributor to *Go, Tell Michelle: African American Women Write to the New First Lady*, Ms. Evans now resides in her hometown of Indianapolis, where she continues to write and remain active in her community and with senior organizations.